YOU ARE A LOVABLE NATIVE KID

Healing What Hurts Inside

Geraldine M. Paul
Registered Psychologist

A Guide For Adults To Read With
Native Children

Copyright © 2023 Geraldine Paul

All rights reserved.

ISBN: 978-1-7388059-0-7

No part of this book may be reproduced or transmitted in any form or by any means, electronic or mechanical, including photocopying, recording or by any information storage and retrieval system, without written permission from Geraldine Paul.

Should errors, omissions, or any consequences arise from using the information in this book, the author cannot accept liability.

DEDICATION

This Book Is Dedicated to Native Children Everywhere.
Creator Made You Exactly Right.

*You are lovable
and you deserve
tender care.*

You are allowed to be your own good friend and ask
for help when you hurt.

Contents

Preface vii

Acknowledgements ix

CHAPTER 1
Native People - Culture and Family 1

CHAPTER 2
Living Away From Birth Family 19

CHAPTER 3
The Gift of Feelings 35

CHAPTER 4
When Someone Hurts You 55

CHAPTER 5
Unhealthy Ways of Expressing Your Hurt
and Upset Feelings 81

CHAPTER 6
Healthy Ways of Expressing Your Hurt
and Upset Feelings 93

CHAPTER 7

When Someone You Know Has an Addiction
to Alcohol, Drugs, Pills, or Other Substances 123

CHAPTER 8

When Someone You Know Passes Away 159

CHAPTER 9

Taking Care of Your Spirit: Your Body,
Your Mind, and Your Heart 221

CHAPTER 10

Conclusion and Being Proud of Your
Native Identity 253

PREFACE

This book is a healing guide for adults to read with Native children. It is intended for kids between 8 and 12 years of age. Children can gain confidence, heal, and embrace their Native identity with a kind and loving adult by their side. Reading together also allows adults time to nurture their children and build even stronger relationships. Further, this book is meant to support adults while navigating through difficult and sensitive conversations with their children.

You can read the chapters in order, starting at Chapter 1, and then work your way to Chapter 10. This book is also written so each chapter can be read independently. You can choose the chapter that will most appropriately help your child now and read it first. You can return to the skipped chapters later.

This book reflects current knowledge and evidence-based practice. The resources the author drew upon are listed at the end of this book.

Please note, this book is intended as *a healing guide* and is not meant as psychotherapy for your child. Your mental health care provider or physician should be consulted when professional psychotherapy is needed.

The author also acknowledges that a one-size-fits-all Indigenous healing guide should not be used for children with certain cognitive and emotional challenges. Please consult with a professional on such matters.

ACKNOWLEDGEMENTS

All the amazing art in this book is by **Loretta Gould**. Loretta is a very talented self-taught Mi'kmaq artist from Waycobah First Nation, Nova Scotia, Canada. Her work beautifully complements the healing intentions of this book. Intentions centre on Native culture, Creator, the Spirits, the land, the animals, and colonization.

I also want to thank **Marina Pigueiras** for helping me format and bring my illustrations to life. Marina is a gifted artist and graphic designer from Calgary, Alberta, Canada. Marina is passionate about her art, consisting primarily of chalk and charcoal drawings.

CHAPTER 1

Being Native is My Superpower

Native People - Culture and Family

Native people live all over the world and have lived in North America long before European and other people came. In this first chapter, I talk about how important it is to know your Birth Family and Native culture. I also explain how every child, including you, deserves to live in a loving and safe home. Let us begin and start learning how your Native identity and culture are important and need to be honoured.

One Native Superpower is Knowing Who You Are!

Learning About Your Native Culture is Important

Native people are also known as *Indigenous People, Indian People, Aboriginal People, Inuit People,* and *First Nations People.* There are also *Métis People*. Métis people have their own culture, and they have **Native** and non-**Native** ancestors. This happens when a **Native** person has children with someone who is non-**Native**. Their children are sometimes referred to as Métis people.

Native people all over the world have a special connection to the land, and many still live on their ancestral land today. Some Native people also speak their Native language.

Ancestral land is where families lived before Europeans and other people came. *Native language* means the language **Native** people spoke long before they spoke English. Native people speak many different **Native** languages. They did not speak English until Europeans came.

Today, Indigenous children and their families also live in cities, towns, farms, inlets, and communities. When Native people live away from their ancestral land, they sometimes lose contact with their **Native** identity. There is good news though. Every **Native** child, including you, belongs to a Clan, a Band, a Nation, or a Tribe. So, if you do not know your **Native** culture, it is never too late to start learning.

You can start learning more about your Native culture by asking these questions:

- Where did my Native family live before European people came? Where do they live today?

- What Native language did my family speak? Do they still speak the same language today?

- What kind of games did the kids play? Remember, there were no video games, TVs, or cell phones back then.

- What kind of clothes did they wear?

- What Native ceremonies did they have? Do they still have the same ceremonies today?

- What kind of homes did they live in?

- What animals did they hunt? Do they still hunt today?

- What food did they eat before European people came? Do you think their food included fry bread, hamburgers, hotdogs, fries, spam, and red wieners?

Learning about your Native family and ancestors is *important* because it helps you understand more about who you are. You are important to this world, and you are allowed to keep learning about your culture. Even if you live on your ancestral land and speak your Native language, you will keep learning new things. You never stop learning!

Say To Yourself:
Learning my Native culture is important because it helps me understand more about myself and my family.

I talk a lot about Creator in this book. Today, Native people refer to Creator in different ways, and they use different names. If you like, you can also say God, Jesus, or another name instead of Creator. What name does your family use when they talk about Creator?

On the following pages, you will see two maps of North America. One map shows several Native tribes in Canada, and the other shows Native tribes in the United States. See if you can locate where your Native parents, grandparents, and great-grandparents are from.

If you do not know, ask an adult. If that adult does not know, ask someone else. Never stop asking. Please note there are other *important* Native tribes not shown on these maps. There was not enough space to include every tribe.

Be Proud of Your Native History and Identity

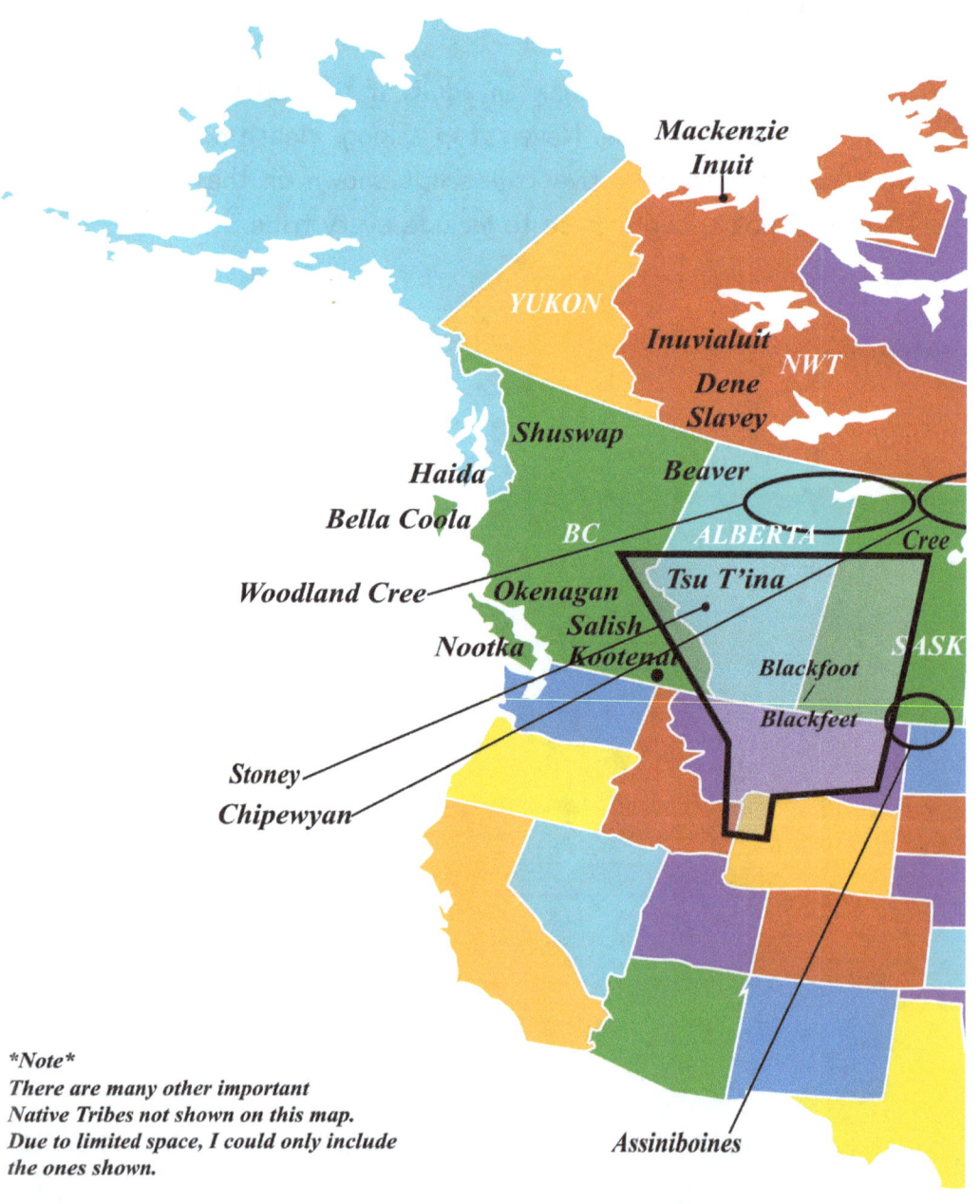

Be Proud of Your Native History and Identity

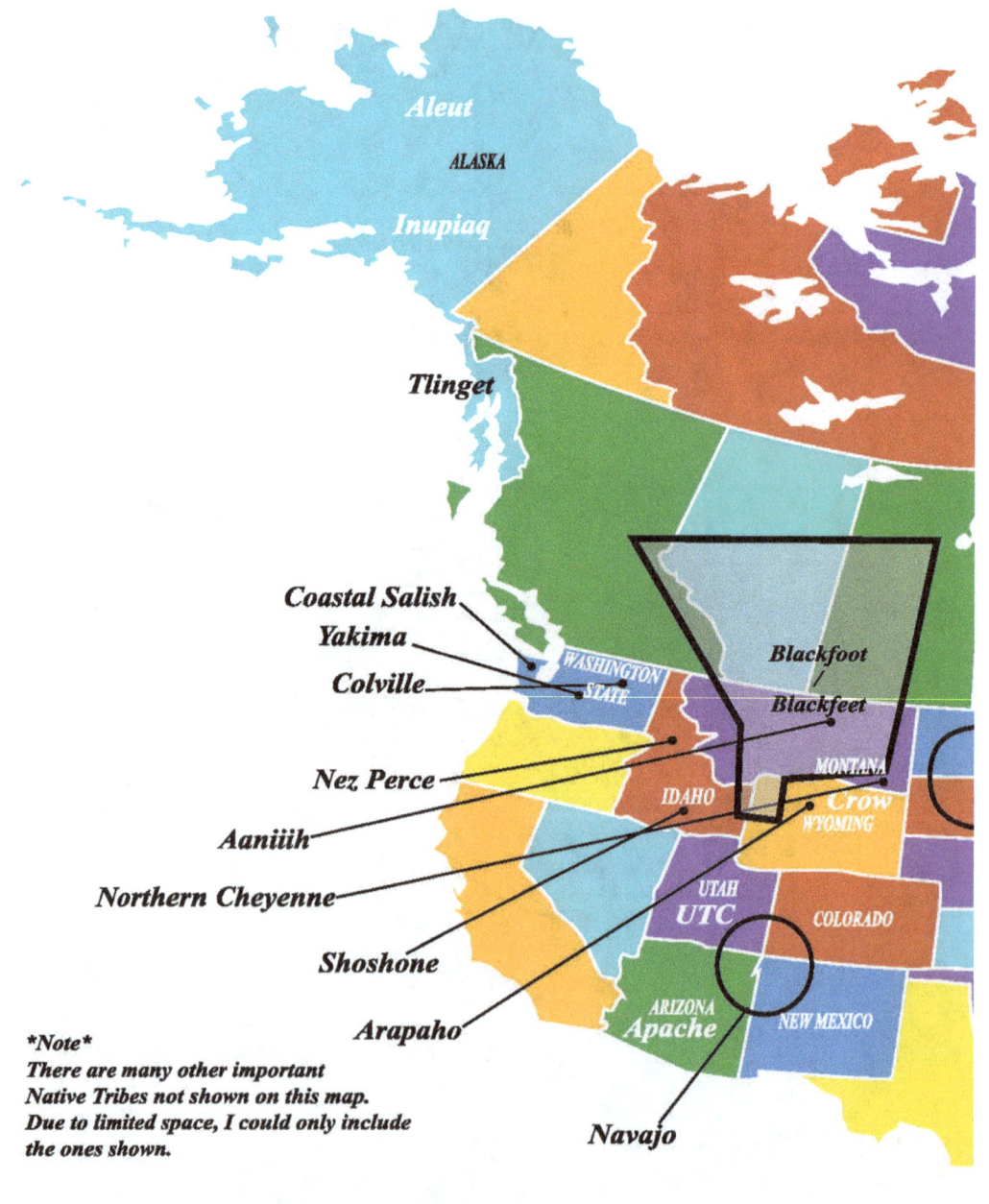

Where is your Native Family From?

UNITED STATES
TRIBES / STATES
By: Geri Paul ©

Next, I talk a little more about two Indigenous groups in North America. One group is from the East, and the other is from the West. Notice what is similar and what is different between these two tribes. Can you find Labrador on the Canada Map? Can you find Montana on the United States Map?

Some Native children are Inuit and live in Labrador, Canada. People from Labrador are very proud of their land and have a special Labrador flag. Native children in Labrador still enjoy many traditional activities like fishing, berry picking, and riding husky dog teams. Kids also love singing, drumming, and riding boats.

Many Labradorian children enjoy modern things, too. They really love skiing, riding bikes, snowmobiles, and quads. Labradorian kids also love using the internet, playing video games, and wearing trendy clothes like brand-name runners and hoodies.

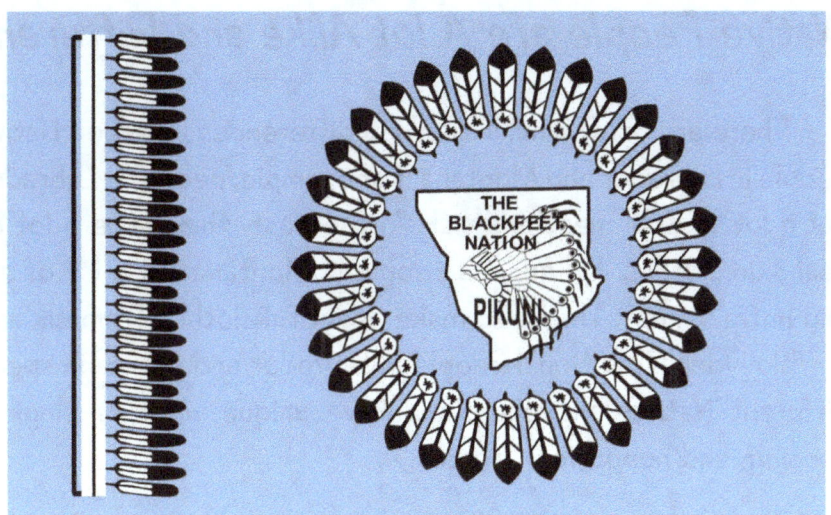

Other Native children are Blackfeet from Browning, Montana, USA. Blackfeet people also have a special flag and are proud of their Native culture. Many Blackfeet children enjoy riding horses, dancing at pow-wows, fishing, and staying in tipis during summer ceremonies.

Some Blackfeet kids love playing basketball, football, running, skateboarding, and attending music concerts. Other kids also love using cell phones, playing computer games, visiting shopping malls, and watching exciting movies while eating popcorn.

Native People are A lot Alike and Different

There are many similarities and differences between Native people in Labrador and Montana. For example, people in Labrador eat a lot of seal meat and fish. In the past, they wore a lot of seal skin clothes. Indigenous people in Montana eat a lot of elk and buffalo meat. They also make beautiful clothes from elk and buffalo hides. Traditional people in Labrador and Montana speak different Native languages, and have unique ways of singing, dancing, and honouring Creator.

Native people in Labrador and Montana are also alike in many ways. For example, in the past, Native people in Labrador and Montana lived off the land. Living off the land means hunting animals and gathering many types of berries, plants, and roots. Both Native tribes also used animal skins and prepared meat and fish similarly. Animal hides were used as warm blankets and for covering homes. Animal hides were also used for making clothes, drums, rattles, and bags. Both tribes also dried and smoked their meat and fish in delicious ways. Some Native people in Labrador and Montana still live off the land today. How would you live off the land?

Whether you are from the East, the South, the West, or the North, Native people everywhere are gifts from Creator. You are a special gift from Creator, too!

Creator loves you and wants you to receive tender love and care (TLC). TLC makes you grow strong and healthy. Creator wants your Birth Family and community to give you this TLC.

When you came from your mother's tummy, you were automatically born into your Birth Family. Your Birth Family includes your mother, father, sisters, brothers, grandmothers and grandfathers, aunties and uncles, and cousins. Sometimes, close friends become family members, too.

Kids can live with many birth relatives, including their parents, grandparents, aunts, and uncles. Some kids also live in more than one home and take turns going back and forth between family homes.

A TLC Home

Every child deserves to live in a family with **TLC**. A *TLC Home* is where adults take good care of their children and one another. There is plenty of tender love and care for everyone in a TLC Home.

> **Say To Yourself:**
>
> Every child deserves to live in a kind and loving home. Including me!

On the next page, you will see what a **TLC Home** looks like. Following this, I outline what a **TLC Home** should *not* look like.

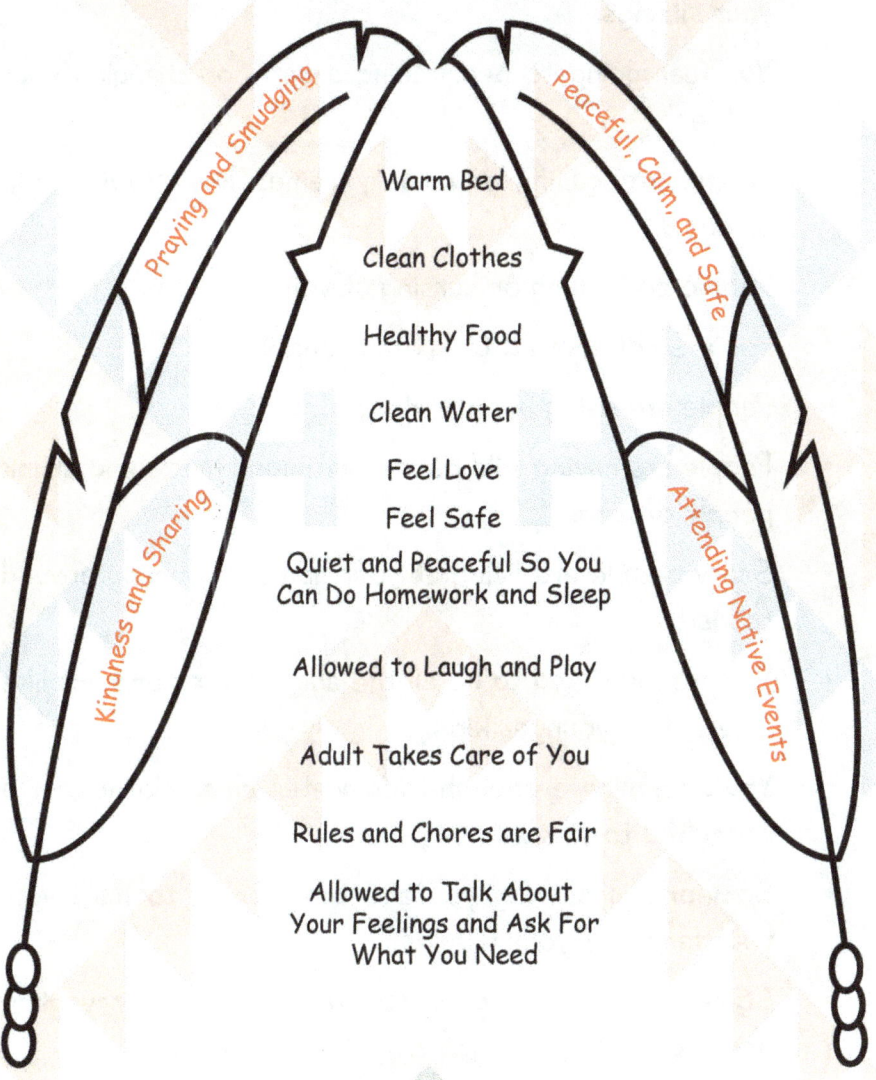

What a TLC Home Should Not Look Like

- Someone is hitting, hurting, or scaring you.
- You are left home without an adult to care for you and your siblings.
- You fear going to bed, taking a bath, or changing your clothes.
- People are calling you nasty names like stupid, ugly, or dumb.
- People are yelling or cursing at you.
- You are not allowed to attend school.
- People are using harmful drugs.
- People are having wild parties with loud music and drunk people around.
- Scary people are living at your home or coming around to visit.
- You are expected to do all the adult chores and act like a parent to younger kids.
- You do not have enough food, water, clean clothes, or a warm bed to sleep in.
- Someone is scaring you and threatening to hurt you, your family, or your friends.
- Someone is touching or trying to touch your vagina, penis, testicles, breasts, or buttocks/behind.
- Someone is looking at or trying to look at your naked body.

- Someone is trying to have you look at or touch their penis, testicles, vagina, breasts, or buttocks/behind.
- Someone is trying to take pictures or videos of your naked body.
- Someone is scaring you into keeping secrets.
- People are putting you down because you are Native.

Say To Yourself:

No one is allowed to hurt me. I am allowed to tell an adult if I feel scared and unsafe.

In the next chapter, I discuss why some children live away from their Birth Family.

CHAPTER 2

Living Away From Birth Family

In the last chapter, we talked about your Birth Family and living in a *Tender, Loving, and Caring Home*. As you probably know, some kids live away from the family they were born into. It is never easy when families separate. In this chapter, I discuss where kids stay when they move, and I explain why some families break apart. I also look at feelings and thoughts kids can have when they live away from their Birth Family.

Places Native Kids Live When Away from Birth Family

- Kids can get *Adopted into a New Family*
- Kids can stay with a *Foster Family*

- Kids can stay with *Relatives they do not know*

- Kids can stay in *Group Homes*

Kids can stay in different places when they move away from their birth relatives. Some kids get adopted and live with new parents and siblings. Children get adopted when they are babies or when they are older. Even teenagers can get adopted.

Kids can also live in foster homes, group homes, or with relatives they know or may not know. Children can stay in these homes when waiting to reunite with their Birth Family or get adopted.

Some kids also move around and live in several foster homes, group homes, or relatives' homes. At times, children can live in these places until they become young adults, which is usually around 18 years of age.

Moving Away From Your Birth Family

Moving away from your Birth Family and living in a new place is never easy. Many thoughts, feelings, and worries usually happen during this time. Remember, whenever a change occurs, it is normal to feel anxious. It is also normal to experience confusing thoughts and feelings when moving to a new place.

Things to Get Used to When Moving

- New People Living in the House

- The Bed, Blankets, and Pillows

- Different Food

- New House Rules

- New Smells and Sounds

- The Size of the House

- New Neighbours

- A New School

- New Students/New Friends/New Pets

If you have recently moved, try to remember it takes time to get used to living in a new place.

Moving to a new house is also the time to practice becoming your own good friend. Treating yourself with extra kindness is a great place to start. For example, ensure you speak kindly to yourself and remind yourself of the following messages:

- This move is not because I did anything wrong. I did not cause my family to break apart.

- I am a lovable kid, and I deserve to feel safe.

- It is **OK** to enjoy things, play, and feel happy in this new house.

- I am allowed to talk about my feelings.

Being your own good friend also means discussing your feelings with someone you trust. Talking can help you feel less alone. Sharing can also help you figure out what is happening inside of you. Some people you may want to talk with include your parents, the adult taking care of you, your family, your case worker, a counsellor, a teacher, or an Elder.

Feelings and Thoughts You May Have When Moving Away From Your Birth Family

Confused	Guilty
Afraid	Lonely
Happy	Anxious
Not Sure	Excited
Feeling Safe	Upset
Sad	Worried

It is also normal to have mixed feelings and thoughts while settling into your new place. For example, it is normal to feel afraid, mad, and confused. You may also feel excited, happy, safe, guilty, and nervous. You may even experience all these feelings at the same time. You are allowed to have all your feelings and think all your thoughts. Remember to share your experiences with someone you trust. Sharing is good!

Say To Yourself:

Even though I do not live with my Birth Family, I am still a lovable kid. I am allowed to have all my feelings and think all my thoughts. I am also allowed to share how I feel and think. Becoming my own good friend and treating myself with kindness are my superpowers!

I will talk much more about healthy ways of expressing your feelings in Chapter 6. In the following pages, I outline why some Native kids live away from their parents and Birth Families.

Some Reasons Native Kids Live Away From Their Birth Families and Parents

If you live away from your Birth Family, it is important to know you did <u>not</u> cause this separation. You could not stop this from happening. Big problems in the world stop families from living together. These difficulties are adult problems, and they are complicated. Many of these challenges started long before you, and even your parents were born. Remember, kids do not cause world problems.

For example, before you were born, Native people were treated very badly by non-Native people and the government (colonizers). This harmful treatment still happens today. Over the following pages, I explain a few *adult problems* that cause some Native parents to live away from their birth children.

Adult Problems In The World

Some Reasons Kids Live Away From Their Birth Family

Hurt Minds, Hurt Hearts, Hurt Spirits, and Hurt Bodies

- Parents feel they are too young to parent well.

- Parents hurt their children, and the home is not safe for kids.

- Parents are sick and live at a hospital, or care facility.

- Parents go to prison.

- Parents or family have addictions.

- Parents or family pass away.

- Laws keep families apart.

- Not enough money to pay bills, and parents are homeless.

- Colonization / Racism.

By: Geri Paul ©

Some Reasons Kids Live Away From their Birth Family

- Adult problems can stop parents from taking safe and loving care of their children. Birth parents sometimes have hurt bodies, hurt hearts, hurt minds, and hurt Spirits. Often, these hurts cannot get fixed right away.

- Some parents, who are hurting and lost, are also unable to work and pay bills.

- Parents who are sick can live in long-term care places or hospitals. They are unable to care for their children.

- Other times, children live away from their Birth Family because their parents or other family members pass away. People pass away from sicknesses like cancer, accidents, old age, and addictions. Parents and family can also pass away for unknown reasons, murder, suicide, or they go missing.

- Some parents lose their way in life and end up breaking the law and going to prison.

- Other parents feel hurt inside and remain unsafe for their children to be around. For example, these parents are unhealthy and can physically hurt their children by hitting them or leaving them alone without care.

- When parents are young, they sometimes believe their children will be happier with other people. They do not feel or believe they are old enough to parent well.

- Parents can also suffer from alcohol or drug addictions. Their addictions stop them from providing a safe *TLC Home* for their children.

Child Services

When parents cannot provide a safe home, Child Services can take their children to safe places. Child Services is the government; its job is to protect children. When children are unsafe, Child Services place children in foster homes, group homes, or with other birth relatives.

Remember, when families break apart, most parents think about their children and still love them very much. Remind yourself of the following message if you live away from your Birth Family.

Say To Yourself:

There are many reasons why I live away from my Birth Family. I did not cause my family to break up. I am a lovable kid who deserves to live in a safe home.

Thinking About Your Birth Family

Children usually have many questions and thoughts when they live away from their Birth Family. Experiencing many feelings is also normal. Remember, all your questions, thoughts, and feelings are important. For example, suppose you have not met your Birth Family. In that case, it is natural to question whether your parents and siblings love you and think about you. It is also OK to question why you do not live with your birth parents. Imagining you have things in common with your relatives and dreaming about meeting is also normal.

For kids who have not seen their relatives for some time, wondering whether they are OK is common. On the next page, are more thoughts kids can have when they live away from their Birth Family. Notice whether you have any of these thoughts.

Do You Have Any of These Thoughts When You Think About Your Birth Family?

- Wondering whether your parents and siblings are safe and happy
- Daydreaming about meeting your Birth Family
- Wondering whether the family you are with now cares about you
- Daydreaming about living together as a family
- Wondering when you will get to see your Birth Family
- Wondering whether you look like your family and have things in common
- Wondering whether your parents love you and think about you
- Wondering whether you did anything wrong, and whether your family is angry or upset with you

Are there other thoughts you have when you think about your Birth Family?

By: Geri Paul ©

Some Things to Remember

- Even though you may not live with your Birth Family, your parents and relatives can still think about you and love you.

- When you live away from your relatives, you can still enjoy doing kid things.

- You are allowed to love and enjoy the family you live with now, and at the same time, you can love and wonder about your Birth Family.

- Daydreaming, wondering, and sometimes worrying about your Birth Family is normal.

- When you remember your Birth Family, it is OK to feel your *good* and *not-so-good* feelings.

I talk a lot more about feelings in the next chapter.

CHAPTER 3

The Gift of Feelings

Every person on earth was born with all their feelings, including you. Your feelings, the *good* and *not-so-good* ones, are gifts from Creator. Do not be afraid of your feelings, you are allowed to accept your gift. Remember, your feelings help you and let you know what is happening inside of you. In this chapter, I include an *Indigenous Feelings Chart* to help you identify and share your feelings. Let us begin by looking at how your feelings are like good friends.

Feelings are Like Good Friends

Your feelings are like good friends. Good friends care about each other and communicate their thoughts and feelings. Like good friends, your feelings communicate with you, too. *Feeling messages* let you know what is happening inside of you and help you take care of yourself. For example, when you feel sad or mad, you can ask for a hug. When you feel hungry and thirsty, you can ask for food and water.

When you pay attention to your feelings, you will receive all kinds of important messages. You will receive messages from your body, your heart, your mind, and your Spirit. You will also receive messages from people. You can become your own good friend by listening to your feelings.

Indigenous Feelings Chart and Being Your Own Good Friend

You can practice being your own good friend by noticing your feelings, and by using your words to let others know how you feel. Your *Good Feelings* can make you feel toasty warm and happy. Your *Not-So-Good Feelings* can make you feel upset and sad. If you get stuck, and cannot always figure out or name your feelings, the *Indigenous Feelings Chart* on the following page can help you.

Say To Yourself:

All my feelings are gifts from Creator. Even my upset feelings help me take care of myself and ask for what I need.

Using Words to Say How You Feel

Let us practice using words to say how you feel. You can say or write your feelings on paper. You can also draw a picture, or you can point to your feelings on the *Indigenous Feelings Chart*.

Practice saying out loud or writing down "*I am feeling*" statements.

I am feeling <u>relaxed</u>

I am feeling <u>happy</u>

I am feeling <u>excited</u>

I am feeling <u>confused</u>

I am feeling <u>tired</u>

I am feeling <u>angry</u>

I am feeling <u>bored</u>

I am feeling <u>anxious and w</u>

I am feeling _____ and _____.

Good job! Keep up the excellent work!

On the following few pages is an exercise to help you get more in touch with your body and feelings. Give the exercise a try. With practice, you will become better and better at understanding and naming your feelings.

Say To Yourself:

With practice, I will become better at figuring out and expressing my feelings.

Exercise

Getting More in Touch with Your Body and Your Feelings

A Guide For The Adult Reader

- Read each step in a soft and calm voice.

- Follow each step, one at a time. Pause before moving forward.

- Take your time, do not rush. Read at a slow speed — you are not running a race.

- Should your child not complete the entire exercise at once, that is OK. You can pick up where you left off later. Remember, this exercise takes much practice.

- Also, remember, when you feel calm, your calm energy spreads to children. When you feel anxious and rushed, your anxiety and rushed energy spreads, too.

- Enjoy yourself! This is a time to build even stronger connections with your child.

- If you like, take turns doing this exercise.

Getting In Touch With Your Body and Feelings Exercise
By: Geri Paul ©

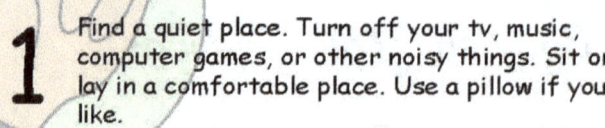

1 Find a quiet place. Turn off your tv, music, computer games, or other noisy things. Sit or lay in a comfortable place. Use a pillow if you like.

2 Now, let's practice your deep breathing. If you like you can close your eyes or keep them open. If you keep your eyes open, find a spot on the wall or ceiling so you can keep looking at it during this exercise.

    a   Breathe in slowly through your nose, all the way down to your belly button. Hold it for two seconds ... one ... two ... now, breathe out slowly through your mouth. Let's practice our deep breathing three more times.

    b   Breathe in slowly though your nose and hold it for two seconds ... one ... two ... now, breathe out very slowly though your mouth. Good Breathing!

    c   Breathe in slowly though your nose and hold it for two seconds ... one ... two ... now, breathe out very slowly though your mouth. Good Breathing!

    d   Last time, breathe in slowly though your nose and hold it for two seconds ... one ... two ... now, breathe out very slowly though your mouth. Good Breathing!

    e   Stay in the same comfortable place and close your eyes. Keep your body very still like a turtle in a shell ... keep breathing slowly and gently. IN and OUT. IN and OUT. Good Breathing!

3 You will now start noticing your body. We will start at the top of your head, and move all the way down to the tips of your cute little toes.

4 Ok, stay relaxed ... and notice the top of your head ... notice the back of your head... notice your eyes ... ears ... nose ... cheeks ... mouth ... and, chin. How does everything feel? Does your head feel heavy, light, dizzy, good, not so good, or are you not sure. Say out loud: "My head and face feel _____."

5 Now, let's notice what you are thinking. What kind of thoughts are going through your mind? Are you thinking happy thoughts, sad thoughts, thoughts of friends, thoughts of food, or thoughts of playing with your friends? Say out loud: "I am thinking _____."

6 Next, let's move to your heart. Place your hand near your heart and notice how it feels. Is your heart beating fast or slow? Does your heart feel happy, excited, nervous, lonely, or relaxed? Say out loud: "My heart feels _____."

Good job at noticing! You are doing great!

7 Now, let's notice how your shoulders, your back, and your tummy feel. Do your shoulders and back feel relaxed or achy? Does your tummy feel warm, happy, nervous, hungry, or hurt? Say out loud: "My shoulders and back feel _____." "My tummy feels _____."

8 Let's notice how your legs feel. Do your legs feel light, heavy, tired, or fidgety (like you want to move)? Say out loud: "My legs feel _____."

9 Let's notice how your feet and toes feel. Do your feet and toes feel tingly, light, heavy, smelly, or wanting to move around? Say out loud: "My feet and toes feel _____."

Great job noticing your feet and toes!

10 You can open your eyes now and take a nice slow deep breath down to your belly button ... and ... breathe out slowly. You can stay laying, or stand up if you like. Give your entire body three gentle shakes. Shake your head, your arms, your tummy, your legs, your feet, and your tail. See if you can shake your toes! Shake all over like a wet puppy who just had a warm soapy bath.

Shake 1 - Shake 2 - and - Shake 3!

Very good job of shaking and noticing your body, thoughts, and feelings. You did great!

The "Getting in Touch With Your Body and Feelings Exercise" can also help you calm down when you feel anxious and worried. I will discuss more about this important topic over the following few pages.

More About Anxiety and Worry

When children feel anxiety and worry, it usually means they feel scared something terrible might happen. When children's worrying starts spinning fast and out of control, it can also become extremely frightening. Even when everything is OK, kids can still have worry wheels and fear something bad might happen. If you ever feel this way, you are not alone.

Many kids, and adults too, have worry wheels. A common worry wheel adults and kids have is about *change*. Change means something will be different. Kids can especially worry when something will not be the same as it was in the past.

What You May Worry About

- When you do not know how new things will turn out.

- When something horrible has already happened, and you worry it might happen again.

- When you hear about bad things happening to other people, and you worry the same things might happen to you.

I will now talk about how your anxiety and worry messages can help you.

Anxiety and Worry Messages

Earlier in this chapter, I talked about how your *good* and *not-so-good feelings* are like friends. It might seem surprising to read that anxiety and worry are also like good friends. Like a good friend, anxiety and worry can let you know when it is time to take extra care of yourself.

Here are two messages anxiety and worry can give you.

Message 1. Your anxiety and worry messages are telling you that something is bothering you, and you need help *figuring it out*. Remember, it is normal to not always know why you feel anxious or worried.

Message 2. Your anxiety and worry messages are saying you need help learning how to *manage or heal* what is upsetting you.

Extra Information About Anxiety

Here is an extra piece of information about anxiety. There are at least two kinds - *good anxiety* and *not-so-good anxiety*.

Good Anxiety

Anxiety is not always a bad thing. Good anxiety occurs when something exciting or new is about to happen. During good anxiety, you can feel excited and nervous at the same time. Also, some anxiety can be helpful because a little worrying can make you work extra hard to do your very best.

An example is feeling excited about moving to a new school and, at the same time, worrying about whether you will make new friends. Another example is feeling excited to play a hockey or basketball game, while worrying about playing your best. You worry because you do not want to let the team down.

Not-So-Good Anxiety

Not-so-good anxiety usually happens when kids worry too much. Kids sometimes worry about bad things happening in the future. They can also worry too much about something that has already happened. Bad anxiety can go around and around inside your mind like a spinning wheel. Here is some more information about worry wheels and anxiety that make kids upset.

- Worry wheels can last a long time and spin out of control.

- Worry wheels can cause kids to feel scared, nervous, frustrated, hyper, sad, sick, overwhelmed, tired, and grumpy.

- Worry wheels can slow down or stop spinning for a while.

- Worry wheels can start up again after stopping or slowing down.

On the following page are more examples of kids' worry wheels. Notice whether you have any of these worries and whether you have more than one worry wheel happening at the same time.

Examples of Kid's Worry Wheels

- Someone will pass away
- That *you* may pass away
- Being left alone
- Not having food
- Not having friends
- People making fun of you
- Someone hurting you
- Having bad dreams
- Will lose your pet
- Bad weather
- Car accidents
- Failing in school
- Not being good enough
- No one will love you
- Someone hurting your family
- Kids looking at you
- Parents are not safe
- Worry about your siblings
- Running out of money
- Not having a home
- Having a sickness
- Parents will not come back

Remember, having worry wheels does not mean you are broken, or you are a bad kid. You do not cause your worrying. Worry wheels means you are a lovable kid who needs help. Everyone, including adults, needs help from time to time.

Help for Worry and Anxiety

You can start getting help by reaching out and talking about what is bothering you. For example, you can begin answering out loud or writing down answers to the following questions. If you like, you can also draw pictures of your worry wheels. Share your answers with the adult helping you.

1. Do you have any of the worry wheels outlined on the last page? If so, which ones do you have?

2. What do you do when you feel worried or anxious? Do you cry ... yell ... lay down ... feel sad ... hit ... scream ... stop eating ... overeat ... feel sick ... feel shaky ... breathe fast or hard ... disobey rules ... stop talking ... or stay alone?

    Is there anything else you do when you feel worried or anxious?

3. Do you have other worry wheels not mentioned already? If so, what else do you worry about?

Important Things to Remember About Your Anxiety and Worry

- Talking about anxiety and worry will *not* make what you are worried about come true.

- Talking about your anxiety and worry will *not* make it worse.

- Talking about your anxiety and worry will help you feel better.

- Practicing your deep breathing will help your worrying slow down. The more you practice deep breathing, the less scary your worry wheels will feel.

- Ask an adult to find help from a professional if your worry wheels do not slow down or go away.

Things to Remember About Your Feelings

- It is OK to not always know how you are feeling. No one is perfect at knowing their feelings all the time.

- Feeling confused about your feelings is normal and happens to everyone now and again.

- Feelings can sometimes change quickly. You can feel happy one minute and feel sad the next minute.

- Feeling the "Not-So-Good Feelings" does not mean something is wrong with you. Good people feel the Good and the Not-So-Good Feelings.

- It is OK to have many feelings at the same time. Feeling happy and sad, mad and glad, or excited and worried, all at once, is normal and OK.

- You can love someone and feel upset with them at the same time. You can feel angry at your parents, for instance, and still love them. This is normal.

Say To Yourself:
Even when I feel my not-so-good feelings, I am still a good and lovable kid.

Say To Yourself:
My feelings are like good friends because they give me messages about what is happening inside me.

In the next chapter, I talk about more ways kids can hurt. I also explain ways you can reach out and ask for help.

For the Adult Reader: Extra Information About Feelings and Emotions

In this book, I use *feelings* and *emotions* as meaning the same thing. However, there is a slight difference between feelings and emotions.

Emotions happen when your body makes actions like hugging or screaming. When you do these things, you are being *emotional*.

Feelings happen in your brain and heart. Your brain tells you that hugging means you are happy. Your heart feels this happiness and excitement.

For example:

You see your dog; you smile and give her a big hug. You feel warm and excited.

Emotions = you are smiling and hugging

Feelings = you feel happy and excited

CHAPTER 4

When Someone Hurts You

People sometimes hurt children in terrible ways. They can hurt your feelings with mean words or scare you with frightening behaviours. Some people also hurt kids by hitting or touching their bodies in wrong and awful ways. If someone is hurting you, tell an adult. You are important, and you should never keep your hurt a secret. In this chapter, I discuss how some kids are mistreated, and I talk about good and bad touch. I also explain ways you can get help if you are hurting.

People Who Hurt Kids

Not all people hurt kids. However, when kids get abused, the people who hurt them include:

- Someone kids know well
- Someone kids know a little
- Someone kids do not know at all (strangers)

People kids know well, who may hurt them, include parents, stepparents, grandparents, aunts, uncles, cousins, sisters, and brothers. Also included are your friends, friends of the family, foster parents, and foster family members. Other people who can hurt kids include babysitters, people at group homes, and support workers.

People kids know a little and strangers, who may hurt them include people online, ministers, priests, fathers, nuns, church brothers and sisters, pastors, and Native ceremonial people, and Native Elders. Also, people who can hurt kids include counsellors, teachers, coaches, people at stores, neighbours, workers at school or daycare, police officers, nurses, doctors, and dentists.

Ways People Can Hurt Kids

By: Geri Paul ©

Your Spirit   *Your Spirit*

HEART
- Calling you bad names like stupid or dumb
- Yelling & swearing
- Making fun of how you look
- Trying to stop you from praying
- Making fun because you are Native
- Saying no one loves you

MIND
- Scaring you
- Threatening to hurt you
- Not letting you read
- Not letting you go to school
- Telling lies about you
- Staring at you
- Saying you are a bad kid

BODY
- Hitting or slapping you
- Pinching you, kicking you
- Burning you, poking you
- Not feeding you
- Not letting you sleep
- Touching your body in uncomfortable ways
- Touching your vagina, breasts, penis, testicles or buttocks (behind)
- Watching you bathe or dress
- Forcing you to use alcohol, drugs, cigarettes, or bad pills

PEOPLE
- Threatening to hurt people you care about
- Saying bad things about people you love
- Keeping you from friends
- Keeping you from family
- Will not let you play, join teams, attend church, or Native events
- Not letting you help others

Ways People Can Hurt Kids

The circle on the last page shows how some people hurt children. People can damage children's hearts, minds, bodies, and Spirits. Some people can also harm the people children love and care about.

Perhaps someone may have hurt or assaulted you already. Some ways you may have been hurt include someone hitting you, slapping you, or kicking you. You may have been locked in places, burned, pinched, poked with things, and not fed. Some people may have also hurt you by touching your vagina, penis, testicles, breasts, or buttocks (behind). As well, someone may have asked you to touch these parts of their body.

People may have also abused and injured you when they asked you to do sexual acts, watch sex videos, or take naked pictures of your body. Tricking you into watching them perform sexual acts, or tricking you into using alcohol and drugs are other ways people may have harmed you.

Seeing someone hurt the people you care about, and hearing people say mean things about them can hurt your heart, too. Yelling at you, scaring you, calling you bad names, making fun of your Native culture, and making fun of your appearance can also harm you. As well, people can abuse you by stopping you from visiting people and going places.

Please tell an adult if you feel hurt or scared. An adult can help you. You deserve to feel safe, and you should never live with abuse. Adults can also find extra support from people who are trained to help children. These people can include Elders and other professionals like doctors, psychologists, social workers, nurses, school counsellors, teachers, and the police.

Say To Yourself:

I am a lovable kid, and I need to feel safe. No one is allowed to hurt my body, my mind, my heart, or my Spirit. If someone hurts me, I am allowed to ask an adult for help.

Being Bullied

Behaving in hurtful ways can hurt people's feelings, thoughts, bodies, and Spirits.

Being bullied is another way children get hurt. Bullying happens when someone tries to harm or scare you on purpose. When kids are bullied, they feel pain and often suffer in silence. **Being bullied is very serious and should never be ignored.**

Bullies can be older kids, younger kids, or kids of the same age. Teenagers and adults also bully kids. If you or someone you know is being bullied, do not keep it a secret. Tell an adult immediately.

If You are Bullying People

Often, kids who bully others are unhappy. If you are bullying people, you must learn how to stop your hurtful behaviours. Maybe you are caught in a cycle of bullying and do not know how to stop. As well, maybe someone bullied you, and now you hurt kids in the same ways you were hurt.

Remember, you are still a lovable kid, and you deserve help. You can learn new ways of expressing your hurt and frustration. You can also learn how to ask for what you want in good ways.

You will feel happier when you treat people with kindness instead of meanness. Ask an adult to help you. Here is one example of how to reach out: you can say, "I need help because I do not want to keep bullying and hurting people."

Bullying Can Happen Almost Anywhere

Bullying can happen almost anywhere and at any time. A few places include:

- At school, on the bus, at the playground

- During sporting events

- Online (on Facebook and other social media places)

- In the church

- At Native events and ceremonies

- At home

- At a friend's or relative's house

What other places can bullying happen?

Bullying Can Happen in Many Ways

Bullying also happens in many ways. People bully children with physical behaviours, hurtful words, and in front of others.

Bullying with physical behaviours includes hitting, kicking, pushing, tripping, ignoring, and throwing things at kids. Making frightening hand and face gestures (like making a fist at you and a scary face) are other ways people bully kids.

Other examples of bullying with physical behaviour include bumping up against kids on purpose, and breaking or taking kids' things (like clothes, money, food, games, and toys). Some kids also get bullied into breaking the law (like stealing or selling drugs) and doing sexual activities.

Bullying with scary and hurtful words includes frightening kids with swearing, yelling, and terrible name calling. Body shaming, telling kids they are ugly, horrible, and they do not deserve to live, are other ways kids are bullied. People also threaten to beat kids up, kill them, or harm their friends or family.

Social bullying occurs when people bully kids in front of other people; like in a classroom, at the playground, or with a group of friends or family. Often kids feel alone, unlovable, scared, and sad when social bullying happens.

Social bullying includes embarrassing kids in front of others, trying to get people to not like them, and leaving kids out of games and activities on purpose. Examples include telling other kids to not play with you, talk to you, and to not pick you for games. Ignoring you and spreading lies about you are other examples of social bullying.

Say To Yourself:

Ignoring bullying will not make it go away. Keeping it a secret will hurt me more. I am allowed to be my own good friend and ask an adult for help.

Some Things to Remember About Bullying

- If someone is bullying you, it is not your fault. You are a lovable kid, and you deserve help.

- If you are the person bullying, you are also a lovable kid, and you deserve help, too.

- Ask an adult you trust to help you. This person could be a parent, a grandparent, an auntie, an uncle, an adult cousin, or an adult brother or sister.

- You can also ask a family friend, an Elder, or a neighbour for help.

- Other people you can ask for help include a doctor, a nurse, a teacher, a social worker, a counsellor, a minister, a police officer, a coach, or a friend's mother or father.

- If the adult you tell does not help, talk to another adult. Be a good friend to yourself and keep asking for help until you get what you need.

Never Give Up! Being Bullied Is Very Serious.

In the following section, I will talk about other ways people can hurt kids.

Good Touch and Bad Touch

Another way people can hurt kids is by touching them in hurtful and scary ways. You are important to this world, and no one is allowed to use bad touch with you. It is very important you know the difference between good touch and bad touch. You must also know how to tell an adult if someone is using bad touch with you.

Good Touch

Good touch feels warm and kind, like getting warm bear hugs and kind gentle dragonfly kisses. Good touch also makes you feel happy and safe. Examples of good touch are friendly "high fives" and friendly pats on the back for doing a good job. Cuddling your dog and rubbing your cat's fluffy fur are also examples of how good touch feels. What are your favourite ways of *receiving* good touch? What are your favourite ways of *giving* good touch?

Bad Touch

Bad touch feels yucky. When bad touch happens, something inside your tummy does not feel right. The touch feels wrong, and kids often feel scared and unsafe when bad touch happens. Kids also feel nervous, and many do not know what to do when someone touches them in bad ways. Remembering how the touch felt also causes a lot of pain and anxiety.

If you were touched in a wrong way (or if someone is still trying to touch you), you might experience some of the following:

- Your tummy feels queasy when the bad touch happens and when you remember it happening.

- You feel aches and pain when the bad touch happens and when you remember it happening.

- Your body shakes or freezes (freeze means unable to move) when the bad touch happens and when you remember it happening.

- You feel numb (numb means not feeling anything) when the bad touch happens and when you remember it happening.

- You feel like your mind is leaving your body when the bad touch happens and when you remember it happening.

- You forget about the bad touch after it happens but remember it later. Sometimes kids do not remember bad touch immediately because remembering is too painful. When this happens, the bad touch memory still gets stored inside your mind, body, and Spirit.

- You have scary dreams that feel like the bad touch is happening all over again.

- It is hard trusting that people will not hurt you again.

- It is hard and confusing telling the difference between good touch and bad touch. For example, many children who experience bad touch can feel nervous and scared when someone gives them kind kisses and warm hugs.

- Some children may even have angry outbursts when someone tries to give them a good touch.

Bad touch hurts children in every way. Kids' bodies, minds, hearts, and Spirits are all injured when they are abused. Never keep bad touch a secret. Tell an adult immediately.

Examples of Bad Touch

- Hitting

- Pushing

- Slapping

- Burning

- Pinching

- Choking or trying to stop you from breathing.

- Rubbing against you in odd or sexual ways.

- Someone touching your penis, testicles, vagina, breasts, or buttocks (behind).

- Asking you to touch their penis, testicles, vagina, breasts, or buttocks (behind).

- Touching or hurting your body with objects.

- Kissing or hugging you in uncomfortable ways.

- Trying to engage you in any sexual behaviour.

Bad touch is not your fault; you did not do anything to cause this. If someone touches you wrongly or did so in the past, remember you are still a lovable kid. You deserve help and can heal from these hurts.

Here are two examples of how you can ask for help. You can say:

- "I need help, someone is touching me in a bad way."

- "I feel scared, someone is trying to hurt me in a wrong way."

I provide more ways you can reach out for help at the end of this chapter.

Say To Yourself:

Bad touch is not my fault. I am a lovable kid, and I am allowed to ask for help when someone tries to hurt me with bad touch.

People Who are Allowed to Touch Your Body

The only people allowed to touch or look at your penis, testicles, vagina, breasts, or buttocks (behind) are those who help you. People who help you include:

- Your doctor or nurse are allowed to touch you when another person is present. For example, your parents or another adult you trust need to be there when you go for check-ups.

- Workers at the hospital doing x-rays and other exams on your body are allowed to touch you. Someone else needs to be there, like your parents or another nurse.

- When you get injured or if you are in pain, your family and other people you trust are allowed to touch you. For example, someone you trust may help and touch your body when you fall and get cut or bruised.

Tricks People Use with Bad Touch

Also, people can sometimes use tricks when trying to touch kids in wrong ways. You must know these so you do not get fooled, and you can tell an adult and get help immediately. In the following section, I mention some of the tricks abusers and molesters use. Remember, there are many other ways bad touch can happen besides the ones I mention.

Tricks People Use With Bad Touch

- People tickle you or play games (like playing doctor, having you sit on their lap), so they can touch your body or have you touch their body in uncomfortable ways.

- Abusers offer you money, gifts, candy, food, video games, clothes, or car rides so they can use bad touch.

- Molesters offer you bonuses (like passing grades or giving you private lessons) so they can use bad touch.

- People trick you into using alcohol or drugs so they can use bad touch.

- Abusers threaten and say if you break the secret, they will hurt you, your friends, and your family.

- Adults use the internet pretending to be kids and ask for your photos. These adults often send fake pictures of other kids and pretend these photos are of themselves. They trick kids into believing they have a true friendship and later ask for bad touch on facetime.

- People use the internet to bully and trick you into believing they will post embarrassing or fake pictures of you.

- Molesters also threaten you and say they will find out where you live if you do not obey them.

More Tricks People Use With Bad Touch

- They say if you love or care about me, you will do what I ask.

- Abusers say you asked for or wanted the bad touch, so it's your fault.

- To use bad touch, people tell you they love you; you are special and beautiful.

- Some molesters say you are making them happy or helping stop their pain.

- People also tell you God or Creator is OK with what they are doing.

- Abusers say bad touch is OK because it will happen just one time.

- Other abusers say bad touch is OK because you are a good friend, a girlfriend, or a boyfriend.

- People say you will hurt or break up the family if you tell.

- People also try to trick you and say you enjoy the bad touch, so it is OK.

- Abusers tell you how lucky you are because they picked you.

- People also threaten that horrible things will happen if you do not obey them.

- Abusers tell you that no one will believe you if you tell what is happening.

By: Geri Paul ©

Feeling Scared to Tell a Bad Secret

Telling an adult about bad touch or another bad secret can feel very scary. For example, you may feel afraid that no one will believe you. Molesters can also threaten to hurt you or your family if you tell their bad secret. As well, you may feel frightened because the abuser, or someone else, blames you for the abuse. **Remember, abuse of any kind and bad touch is never your fault.** Kids can also feel afraid to share because they do not want to cause trouble, hurt someone's feelings, or break up their family.

Sadly, children can stop asking for help when they are punished for telling the truth, and the adult they told does not believe them. For example, sometimes an adult will beat or hit kids, call them liars, or pretend they did not hear what was shared. Some adults also accuse kids of making up a story that is not true.

Feeling scared to tell a bad secret also happens when an adult makes excuses for the abuser. Excuses include saying the person who touched or hit you did not mean it. They can say the abuser was drunk, high, or stressed out. The adult can also say you asked for it because you should not dress and behave as you do, and it will not happen again.

Remember, all these excuses are wrong, and the adult should not punish, blame you, or make up reasons for the abuser's behaviours. An adult must help you and support you because bad touch is always wrong, and it is never your fault.

Also, please remember, if the adult you reach out to makes up excuses and do not help you, tell someone else. Never stop asking until you get the help you need. **Abuse and bad touch are never OK, and never your fault.**

Ways You Can Get Help

Always tell an adult if someone is hurting you or trying to use bad touch. If you feel scared or too shy to speak, ask for help by writing a note or drawing a picture. Give the note or drawing to an adult you trust.

The adult can also request an Elder or another professional to help you. A *professional person* is someone like a doctor, a psychologist, a teacher, a school counsellor, or a social worker. Professional people are trained to help children in these situations. They see many kids who also experience abuse and bad touch. Professionals care and know every kid deserves help, including you! The following are examples of what you can say when you reach out.

How You Can Ask for Help

"I need to talk because someone is hurting me"

"I feel scared"

"I am hurt, and I was touched in a bad way"

"Someone is scaring me into keeping bad secrets"

"Someone is asking me to do things that make me feel bad and uncomfortable"

"Someone is hurting my body"

"I am scared to talk about what hurts me"

"I am scared to talk about what makes me feel bad"

"I feel sad because I am being hurt"

"I do not feel safe at home" "I do not feel safe at ___"

"I was told to not talk about being hurt because bad things will happen to me and my family"

"The person hurting me said if I tell, child welfare will take me and my siblings away, and it will be my fault"

"I am being hurt and afraid to tell what is hurting me"

"Someone has done things to me that feel wrong"

Things To Remember When Someone Is Hurting You

- Never keep your hurt a secret.

- You can ask for help by writing a note, drawing a picture, or talking to an adult.

- People you can reach out to, or give your note or drawing to, include a parent, grandparent, aunt, uncle, teacher, counsellor, police officer, doctor, or another adult you trust.

- Abusers and molesters use many tricks to hurt and scare kids. Abuse and bad touch are never your fault. Even if you were tricked into doing horrible things, you are not to blame for abuse or bad touch.

- If the adult you reach out to does not help you, keep asking other people until you get the help you need.

Say To Yourself:

I am a lovable kid, and I am allowed to tell an adult if someone is scaring me, hurting me, touching me, or trying to touch me in bad ways.

You did a fantastic job reading this chapter!
Keep up the excellent work!

In the next chapter, I discuss *unhealthy ways* kids can express their hurt and upset feelings. Later in Chapter 6, I outline *healthy ways* you can communicate your frustration and pain.

Upset Feelings Sometimes Erupt In Hurtful Behaviours

Yelling   Disobeying Rules   Hitting

Breaking Things   Throwing   Spitting   Stop Speaking

Bullying   Hurting Yourself   Smoking   Drinking Alcohol

Stealing   Lying

Hurt

Sad

Lonely

Confused

Frustrated

Mad

Angry

Jealous

By: Geri Paul ©

CHAPTER 5

Unhealthy Ways of Expressing Your Hurt and Upset Feelings

Kids, teenagers, and adults all make mistakes from time to time and show their upset feelings in hurtful ways. When you make mistakes, it does not mean you are a bad kid. You are still lovable and important. In this chapter, I invite you to look closely at unhealthy ways you may express your hurt and frustration. I begin by discussing how kids' outbursts may look like an erupting volcano of behaviours.

Upset Feelings and Hurtful Behaviours

A buildup of "Not-So-Good Feelings" can sometimes erupt like a volcano. The eruption can cause hurtful behaviours toward people, yourself, animals, things, and property. Erupting volcanoes can hurt and scare the people you love and care about the most. You can hurt and scare your siblings, parents, grandparents, cousins, best friends, and many others. You can even end up hurting yourself and destroying property and important things.

Harmful outbursts also hurt people in different ways. You can harm people's minds, hearts, bodies, and Spirits.

Notice whether your feelings sometimes come out like those shown in the erupting volcano picture. Should your Not-So-Good Feelings come out in unhealthy ways, this does not mean you are a terrible unlovable kid.

How do You Think People Might Feel When Your Upset Feelings Erupt in Hurtful Behaviours?

When you erupt with hurtful behaviours it usually means:

- You are hurting inside, and your hurt comes out in harmful actions.

- You have not learned how to manage your unhealthy outbursts yet.

- You have not learned how to talk about your upset feelings in respectful ways.

- You are frustrated, scared, and feel like no one cares enough to listen to you.

- You feel unloved and feel like a bad kid.

Say To Yourself:

I am *not* allowed to hurt people, myself, animals, or damage things when I feel upset. Instead, I will learn to express my feelings in healthy ways.

Paying attention to your mistakes is not easy because uncomfortable feelings can arise. For example, you may feel sad, mad, guilty, hurt, or frustrated. Remember, it is OK to experience these feelings when you look at your mistakes. Experiencing uncomfortable feelings is normal.

Also, remind yourself that expressing yourself in hurtful ways does not mean you are a terrible kid. Even when you make mistakes, you are still lovable. It is your harmful behaviours that are not good.

It is important to learn from your mistakes and to keep trying your best. This way, you can stop making the same errors over and over.

Say To Yourself:

I must look closely at my unhealthy behaviours. Understanding my outbursts will help me learn new ways of expressing my feelings. I am still a lovable kid, and I will keep trying my best.

The Good News About Looking Closely at Erupting Volcanoes

You can learn important lessons when you look closely at your erupting volcanos. Four of these lessons include the following.

Lessons You Can Learn by Looking at Your Erupting Volcanoes

1. You can see that everyone makes mistakes. Creator did not make people to be perfect. It is important to remember that making mistakes means you are a normal kid.

2. You get a chance to take responsibility for your actions. You can say, "I made a mistake, and I am sorry." Apologizing from your heart shows you want to stop your harmful behaviours.

3. You get a chance to ask for help. When you have difficulty managing your upset feelings, you can learn ways to ask for help. You can say, "I am upset, I need help, I need a hug, I need to talk, or I need to get some fresh air."

4. You get a chance to practice healthy behaviours. You can stop making the same hurtful behaviours and replace them with healthy ones.

Unhealthy Ways of Expressing Feelings

You can start controlling your unhealthy behaviours by noticing your actions when you are upset and hurt. Looking closely at your outbursts will not make them worse; and it will not cause them to happen more often. Looking carefully at your unhealthy behaviours means you are *brave*.

Unhealthy Ways of Expressing Feelings

Let us now look closely at whether you behave in any of the following ways when you feel upset.

Read each square and answer, "YES, I behave this way", or answer, "NO, I do not behave this way when I feel upset."

Hitting, punching, slapping people	Hitting or hurting yourself	Throwing things
Smoking cigarettes or using alcohol or drugs	Swearing, yelling	Breaking things
Taking people's things	Taking your upset feelings out on other people or animals	Lying

Read each square and answer, "YES, I behave this way", or answer, "NO, I do not behave this way when I feel upset."

Making fun of how people talk or look Making fun of yourself	Calling yourself or other people names like dumb, stupid, ugly	Not asking for help Staying silent Staying alone
Saying mean things about someone when they are not around	Not listening to the rules at home, at school, or in other places	Eating too little or eating too much
Bullying	Spitting, biting people	Skipping school

Behaving in hurtful ways can hurt people's feelings, thoughts, bodies, and Spirits.

By: Geri Paul ©

We talk a lot more about replacing hurtful behaviours with healthy ones in the next chapter. For now, remember it takes patience and practice to become good at changing old behaviours. With patience, you will learn how to control your outbursts, and with practice, it becomes easier.

> **Say To Yourself:**
> I am a lovable kid, and I can learn healthy ways of expressing my upset feelings. With patience and practice, it gets easier.

Also, remember, when you slip back into old behaviours, remind yourself to never give up, and keep trying hard. Tell yourself, "it is normal to make mistakes and fall back sometimes. I can do this"!

You did a good job noticing your unhealthy behaviours!
Keep up the great work!

In the next chapter, I talk about ways you can express your hurt and upset feelings in healthy ways.

CHAPTER 6

Healthy Ways of Expressing Your Hurt and Upset Feelings

Children often feel sad when they hurt the people they love and care about. I am sure you feel the same way when you hurt someone. The good news is you can learn from your mistakes and stop harmful behaviours. In this chapter, I discuss how you can calm your body down and use good words to express your feelings. I start by talking about how you can ask for what you need in kind and considerate ways.

Expressing Your Upset Feelings with Good Communication

Creator gave everyone the ability to communicate. You were born with a whole bunch of built-in communication skills. For example, when you were a tiny baby and felt hungry or had a belly ache, you communicated by crying. When you wanted love and affection, you also expressed it by letting others know you enjoyed their warm snuggles. When you were tired, you had sweet baby yawns and communicated you needed sleep. I am sure you still have sweet yawns today. Remember, no matter how old you become, you are still allowed to cry, snuggle, and express your needs.

Now that you are older, you can also use your words to ask for what you want and need.

Here are a few good ways older kids, like you, can communicate:

- Speak with kindness and talk from your heart.

- Consider people's feelings before you speak and act.

- Use good manners, like saying please, thank you, and waiting your turn when you want something.

- Use your words, art, or writing to let others know how you feel.

As you know, kids do not always communicate in kind and considerate ways. The erupting volcano picture from the last chapter shows how children may express their hurt, sadness, and frustration. For example, kids can hit, yell, hurt themselves, stay alone, and damage things. I will talk more about how you can fix these mistakes later. For now, I want to share a few more cool things about communicating.

Some Other Really Cool Things About Communicating

You communicate with yourself, other people, and with Creator. You can also communicate with animals, trees, plants, and medicines. Animals communicate with one another and with people, too.

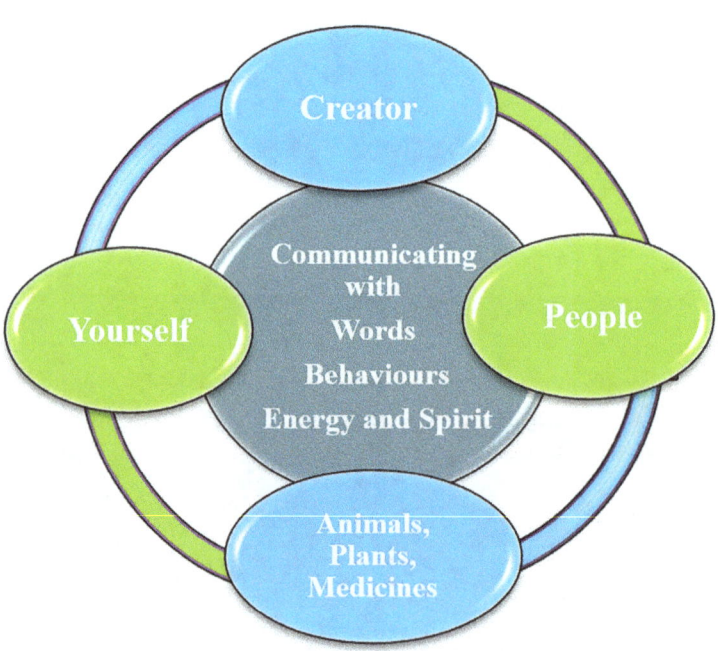

Even when you do not speak you communicate. For example, when you make funny faces and dance in silly ways, you communicate and let others know you are enjoying yourself and feeling happy. People pick up happy energy from your body and Spirit when you feel glad.

- Also, people pick up sad energy from your body and Spirit when you feel low and blue.

- Remember, you communicate through your senses. Senses let you see, hear, smell, feel, taste, and touch things.

Some Ways People Use their Senses to Communicate

- Singing and dancing
- Smudging and praying
- Drawing, looking at art, and walking in nature
- Talking to Creator, yourself, people, and animals
- Hugging, giving gifts, helping people

What are your favourite ways of communicating?

- Watching and making videos
- Reading and writing
- Eating and drinking
- Wearing certain clothes
- Making your body smell good

Talking to Yourself

You also communicate with yourself all the time by talking to yourself. Every single person was born with a little voice inside of them. This voice is called your *inner voice* and you use it with your self-talk.

Your self-talk is great because you can use it at any time and in different ways. You can speak in your mind or *out loud* when it is OK. You do not want to talk out loud when someone else is talking or if you are in a ceremony or class.

Communicating with yourself is also great because you can be your own good friend and figure things out. For example, self-talk can help you figure out how to calm yourself down and relax when you feel mad or frustrated.

How to Use Your Inner Voice When You Feel Upset

You can use your self-talk to figure out and express your not-so-good feelings.

> **Say To Yourself:**
> I can be my own good friend and use my inner voice to help myself. My self-talk can help me calm down and relax.

For example, when you feel like yelling, throwing, kicking, hurting yourself or someone else, you can practice using your self-talk to cool down. You can talk to yourself and say the following:

- "Stop! Take a deep breath ... breathe ... and slow down."

- "I do not need to yell or erupt right now."

- "I got this! I have a calm talking voice, and I am allowed to use it."

- "I will use kind words and say how I am feeling, and I will not erupt in hurtful ways."

I will talk more about self-talk later. For now, you can practice listening to how your inner voice sounds. Try the "Noticing Your Self-Talk Exercise" on the following two pages.

Noticing Your Self-Talk Exercise
By: Geri Paul

Ask someone to read these instructions to you in their calm voice. The reader should read each step, one at a time. Ensure your listener gets enough time to finish one step before moving to the next.

Step 1 Be very quiet. Turn off all noise like the TV/music/video games/cellular phones.

Step 2 Sit in a comfortable position, or you can lie down. You can close your eyes if you like.

Step 3 Take a deep breath through your nose, right down to your belly button. Count to five as you breathe in. 1-2-3-4-and 5. Hold your breath in your belly and count to three. 1-2-and 3. Now, let your breath come out very slowly through your mouth. Count to five as you breathe out. 1-2-3-4-and 5.

Step 4 Practice Step 3 two more times. Remember to breathe in deeply, right to your belly button and breathe out slowly.

Step 5 Stay calm and keep breathing softly. Now, close your eyes and listen to the conversation inside your mind. Keep breathing slowly and softly. Be very quiet. Ask yourself, "What am I saying to myself right now?"

Step 6 Be patient with yourself. It may take a few tries to notice your self-talk. Stay relaxed and listen to what you are saying in your mind. Keep breathing softly and slowly.

Step 7 Tell the reader what talk is happening inside your mind. You can start by saying, "I noticed I was telling myself ...." Keep breathing softly and continue sharing in your calm voice. Talk for as long as you like. Your listener can listen without interrupting or going on their phone. Tell the talker, "Good noticing" when they are finished speaking.

Step 8 When you are finished sharing, you can open your eyes and stay lying down or stand up. Give your entire body three gentle shakes. Shake all over like a tree shaking off leaves. Shake 1 ... Shake 2 ... and ... Shake 3.

Practice this exercise every week until it becomes easy.

Good job at noticing your self-talk. You did great!

Choosing Good Words

Your Words are another Superpower

We will now look at some **good words** you can use when talking to yourself and others. Your words are a *superpower* because the words you choose really influence how people think and feel. Kind words can warm people's hearts, and mean words can really hurt them. Kind words also help people heal when they feel sad and hurt.

Also, the words you choose when talking to yourself are a superpower. It is so critical to use *kind words* when you speak to yourself. Do not talk to yourself in bad ways by using negative messages.

Using Your Calm Talking Voice

Using a *calm talking voice* is also great. When you are upset, it is not cool to speak in a loud and angry voice. You can hurt and scare people. Remember, you do not need to yell, scream, swear, mock, or put people down. When you feel upset, speaking calmly and using good words are always best. Below are examples you can use. Practice now, and you will be prepared for when you feel upset.

Read each sentence out loud and practice using your calm talking voice.

> I feel angry
>
> I feel mad
>
> I feel sad
>
> I feel lonely
>
> I feel hurt
>
> I feel tired
>
> I feel left out
>
> I feel scared
>
> I am not sure how I feel
>
> I feel jealous

Using your calm voice and choosing good words gets easier with practice. Keep trying hard and never give up. You can do it!

Using Good Words to Ask for Help

Every person in the world needs help from time to time. Remember, you are important to this world, and you, too, deserve help. The more you practice asking for what you need, the easier it becomes. Below are examples of sentences you can use when asking for what you need.

Read each sentence out loud and practice using your calm talking voice.

> I need a hug
>
> I need to talk and vent
>
> I need alone time
>
> I need time to cool down
>
> I am not sure what I need. Can you help?
>
> I need you to just sit with me
>
> I need to talk about my feelings
>
> I need to talk about feeling afraid

What other ways can you ask for help?

When You Feel Upset, Notice Your Body Talk

So far, we talked about how you can express your upset feelings by:

- Talking kindly to yourself and listening to your *inner voice*.

- Speaking in your *calm talking voice*.

- Choosing *good words* when you talk to yourself and other people.

- Using good words to ask for help.

Next, we look at how your **body** talks to you. Your body talk is amazing! Like your mind, your body also lets you know when you feel frustrated, disappointed, hungry, sick, tired, scared, and hurt. When you listen to your body, you can learn to cool down and avoid hurtful outbursts. Remember, it is important to learn from your mistakes and stop repeating the same harmful behaviours. Listening to your body talk can help with this.

THE GOOD NEWS IS YOU CAN LEARN TO NOTICE
YOUR BODY TALK AND **STOP HURTFUL** BEHAVIOURS
FROM HAPPENING.

Say To Yourself:
I can learn to express my hurt and upset feelings in healthy ways. The more I practice, the better I will notice how my body talks to me.

On the next page are examples of how your body may talk to you *before* an outburst happens. Notice whether your body gives you any of these red flags when you feel upset.

Body Talk Before an Outburst

Does your body give you any of these messages before an outburst?

Shaking

Clinch your teeth

Hands make a fist

Hands get ready to throw things

Mouth gets ready to yell, say mean words, swear, spit, or bite

Feet get ready to kick, stomp, or run away

Does your body give you any other messages before an outburst?

By: Geri Paul ©

You can get more in touch with your *body talk* by practicing the exercise below.

> ## Exercise: Noticing Your Body Talk When You Feel Upset
>
> *By: Geri Paul*
>
> - Ask someone to read these instructions to you. Your reader should read the instructions slowly, one at a time, in a calm voice.
>
> - Turn off all noise and find a relaxing place to sit or lay down. You can close your eyes if you like.
>
> - Take your time, there is no need to rush.
>
> - Take slow deep breaths, all the way to your belly button. Deep breathe throughout this exercise.
>
> - Let's begin.

Bring up a memory of when you felt upset or angry. Think of a time when someone would not give you what you wanted (like the TV remote, a turn playing a game, or a snack). Take your time and notice the memory. Share the memory out loud. Explain what made you upset? Explain how you felt at that time?

1. Keep remembering the memory and start noticing how your body felt during that time. Start at the top of your head and notice how your head feels when you remember feeling upset or angry. Notice your mouth as well. Take a deep breath and let it out slowly through your mouth. Good work!

2. Move to your neck ... shoulders ... arms ... and hands. Notice how they feel when you remember being upset or angry. Take a deep breath and let it out slowly. Good job!

3. Now, notice your chest ... heart ... and tummy. Notice how they feel when you remember being upset or angry. Take a deep breath and let it out slowly. Very good!

4. Next, move to your legs ... and feet. Notice how they feel when you remember being upset or angry. Take a deep breath and let it out slowly. You are doing great!

5. Take three deep breaths to your belly button and let them out slowly. One deep breath ... Let it out slowly... and ...Take another deep breath ... Let it out slowly ... and ... Take a last deep breath ... Let it out slowly. Great breathing!

6. Say to yourself, "I will move away from the angry or upsetting memory now." Keep breathing slowly and softly.

7. Share out loud what you noticed about your body when you remembered the memory. Answer these questions: was your body getting shaky or getting ready to cry or throw something? Were you getting ready to hit, kick, run away, or hide? Did you feel yourself getting ready to yell, say mean words, or hurt yourself? What else did you notice?

8. To the reader, remind your listener to deep breathe again once they finish sharing. Check-in and ensure they are not distressed.

9. Tell your listener: "You did an awesome job with noticing your body!"

Practice this exercise every week until it becomes easy.

Cooling Down Activities

Over the following few pages, I discuss some *cooling-down* activities you can practice when you feel yourself about to erupt. These include:

- Deep breathing

- Moving your body and self-care

- Writing and drawing out your feelings

- Taking a time-out

- Using your imagination

- Becoming your own good friend

- Talk to Creator

Upset Feelings Sometimes Erupt In Hurtful Behaviours

Yelling   Disobeying Rules   Hitting

Breaking Things   Throwing   Spitting   Stop Speaking

Bullying   Hurting Yourself   Smoking   Drinking Alcohol

Stealing   Lying

Hurt

Sad

Lonely

Confused

Frustrated

Mad

Angry

Jealous

By: Geri Paul ©

When You Feel Upset, Practice Deep Breathing

Let us start by learning how to breathe deeply. Take a deep breath when you feel mad, sad, worried, hurt, lonely, frustrated, or confused. Tell yourself, *"Stop. Take a deep breath and calm down. I've got this!"* Here is a deep breathing exercise you can practice right now.

Deep Breathing Exercise

1. Breathe in good thoughts through your nose, deep in your tummy, all the way to your belly button. Count to five as you breathe in.

2. Hold your breath by your belly button, and count to three.

3. Now, very slowly, breathe out bad energy and bad thoughts, through your mouth. Count to five as you breathe out.

4. Say to yourself, "I did a good job. I will be OK."

5. Repeat the steps above three more times.

When You Feel Upset, Do Cooling Down Activities Like the Following

Move Your Body Activities

- Ride A Bike
- Play Soccer
- Mow The Lawn
- Pow Wow Dance
- Ride a Horse
- Play Basketball
- Walk
- Hip Hop Dance
- Exercise
- Skate
- Jump Rope
- Go Fishing
- Shoot Pucks
- Play with your Dog
- Go Hunting

By: Geri Paul ©

What Activities Do You Enjoy?

More Activities to Help Your Body Relax and Cool Down

- Read
- Sing
- Smudge
- Play Music
- Walk in Nature
- Take a Nap
- Give Yourself a Hug
- Jump Rope
- Watch Funny Videos
- Play With Toys
- Pray
- Dance

By: Geri Paul ©

When You Feel Upset, Write or Draw Your Feelings

Writing about or drawing your feelings is very helpful. Remember, noticing your upset feelings will not make them worse. You can express your feelings by drawing a picture. Explain your picture to someone. You can also write a letter to yourself or someone else, explaining how you feel. Writing in a private journal or diary is also a great idea.

If you do not know exactly how you feel, that is OK. You are allowed to express and write about the *not knowing* feelings, too. You can also use the *Indigenous Feelings Chart* to help you.

When You Feel Upset, Take a Time-Out

You can take a time-out when you feel your body getting upset. Everyone needs a breather every now and again.

There are many things you can do in time-out. You can do the cooling-down activities shown earlier. Also, you can let your feelings happen during your time-out. It is perfectly fine to cry if you feel like it. Should you feel uncomfortable crying in front of people, you can go to your bedroom or another safe place. Crying is a good thing because it helps your hurt and frustrations come out. Your tears are healing. Keeping your tears inside can end up hurting you more.

When You Feel Upset, Use Your Imagination

Another great gift you were born with is your imagination. When you feel upset, you can go into your pretend world and escape to any place you wish. You can go somewhere brand new or visit a place you know. Escaping in your mind for a little while is perfectly fine. Here are some ways you can use your imagination.

When You Feel Upset, Pretend You Are an Animal

You can also use your imagination and pretend you are an animal. What animal would you choose? Would you prefer a rabbit, a tiger, a lion, a turtle, a bear, a cat, a dog, or a bird? I love pretending I am a bird, flying high in the sky, and enjoying all of Creator's beauty.

You can pretend you are a bird, too, if you like. Imagine you see the hills, the ocean, and wildflowers everywhere. Imagine feeling the warm breeze on your bird face and smelling the fresh air. Pretend you hear other birds singing, and you are tasting the salty air. Feel your body relaxing. Enjoy feeling free as you glide with the wind under your wings. Keep flying for as long as you like. This is *your* pretend world!

When You Feel Upset, Become Your Own Good Friend

When you notice your body getting ready to behave in unhealthy ways, let yourself become your own good friend. Talk nicely to yourself and stop any bad self-talk. For example, when you feel upset or frustrated, never call yourself bad names like stupid, dumb, ugly, or useless. Never swear at yourself or tell yourself you are a bad kid. Instead, tell yourself good messages like the following.

> **Say To Yourself:**
> I am a good person, and I am my own good friend. I can cool down. I will be OK. I've got this!

Becoming your own good friend also means asking for help and talking with someone when you feel upset. For example, when you feel mad or hurt, you may ask the person you love for a hug. You may also ask someone to talk or walk with you.

When you are sad or mad, you might also feel alone and like no one cares about you. It might also seem like no one in the world understands your feelings. During these times, become your own good friend. Remind yourself that even when you are alone and feeling sad or mad, there are people who care about you and want to help you.

> **Say To Yourself:**
> When I feel mad or upset, I am still a lovable kid. There are people who care about me and who want to help me. I am allowed to be my own good friend and ask for help.

When You Feel Upset, Talk to Creator

Remember, Creator wants to help you. He is always there and loves hearing from you. Speak to Creator like you would talk to a friend.

In this chapter, we talked about healthy ways to express your upset feelings. In the next chapter, I talk about how people with addictions can also upset kids by causing them a lot of hurt and damage.

CHAPTER 7

When Someone You Know Has an Addiction to Alcohol, Drugs, Pills, or Other Substances

Children can experience much hurt when someone in their family has an addiction. If you know someone addicted to alcohol, drugs, pills, or other substances, you may feel confused, hurt, scared, embarrassed, or mad. In this chapter, I will talk about what being addicted means. I also explore how good people can get trapped in an addiction cycle. As well, I will discuss problems you and your family may be experiencing if someone you know is lost in addiction.

Understanding Addictions and Hurt

Most people with addictions want to turn their lives around and change their unhealthy behaviours. Many people, who try hard, can stay quit and live good *sober* lives. Living a sober life means the addicted person no longer uses alcohol, drugs, pills, and other harmful substances. Sadly though, many people end up in a *cycle of addiction*. A cycle of addiction means the person quits for a while then starts *using* all over again. They keep stopping and starting.

If someone you know is lost in addiction, you may also find yourself in a cycle of feeling disappointed and hurt. That is, every time a promise to quit is broken, you might start feeling disappointed and hurt all over again.

When an addicted person breaks their promises to stay sober, you may lose hope and give up believing they will quit. Remember, it is normal to feel hurt and discouraged. It is also normal to question why the addicted person keeps *using* when they know it hurts many people, including themselves.

Addictive Substances are Powerful

Alcohol, drugs, harmful pills, and other addictive substances are dangerous. These *powerful* substances act like a boss *of* many good Native people. Quitting is hard because **The Alcohol and Drug Boss**, or **The Alcohol and Drug Spirit**, tells people to keep using. Quitting also becomes extra hard for many Native people because they face more problems than non-Natives. I will talk about this topic later.

Other Upset Feelings

In addition to disappointment and hurt, you may feel many other upset feelings when you know someone with an addiction. For example, you may feel frustrated, sad, alone, helpless, unloved, or unsafe. You may also experience a mix of *opposite* feelings. That is, you may find yourself loving the person with an addiction, and at the same time, you may feel terribly upset and mad at them. You may also believe the addicted person is selfish and cares only about themselves and getting drunk or high.

When the addicted person is a close family member (your mother, father, grandparent, brother, sister, aunt, uncle, or cousin, for instance), some kids feel embarrassed. Sometimes kids wish they did not belong to their family at all. Kids can also feel so upset and hurt, they never want to see or hear from their addicted relatives again.

Thinking or feeling like any of the above does not mean you are a terrible or bad kid. You may be surprised to learn all these thoughts and feelings are normal. Knowing someone with addictions is complicated. Many of the *not-so-good feelings* happen because a lot of damage and hurt takes place.

Addictions Cause Suffering for Everyone
Addictions Bring About

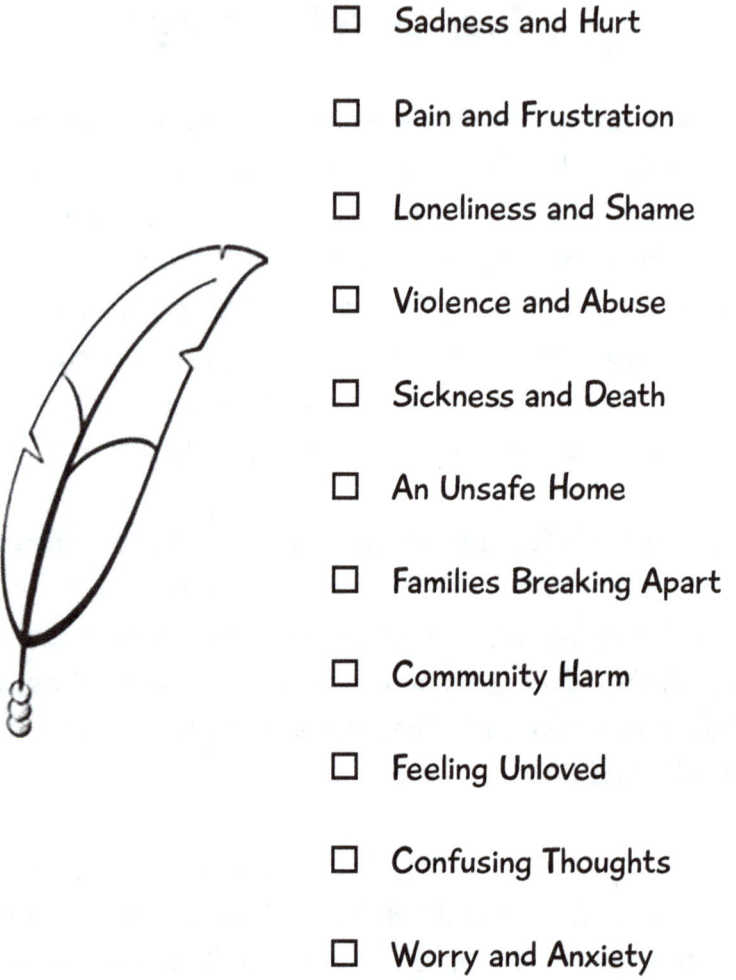

- ☐ Sadness and Hurt

- ☐ Pain and Frustration

- ☐ Loneliness and Shame

- ☐ Violence and Abuse

- ☐ Sickness and Death

- ☐ An Unsafe Home

- ☐ Families Breaking Apart

- ☐ Community Harm

- ☐ Feeling Unloved

- ☐ Confusing Thoughts

- ☐ Worry and Anxiety

Talking About Addictions

If someone close to you suffers from an addiction, it is important to talk about your feelings. Use the *Indigenous Feelings Chart* to help you express what is happening inside of you. If you like, you can ask an adult to talk about their feelings first. You can share once they finish.

If you are not ready to talk, you can always point to how you feel on the *Indigenous Feelings Chart.* You can also write or draw your feelings in a book. Remember to share your writing or pictures with an adult you trust.

To help you start, I will list a few questions on the next page. You can begin by answering the questions you are most comfortable talking about first. As well, try to answer the feelings questions with *"I feel"* statements. For example, "I feel sad and lonely when I think about my mother." Remember, all your feelings are important, so keep talking for as long as you need.

Questions to Help You Start Talking About Knowing Someone With an Addiction

Who do you know with an addiction? Look at the *Indigenous Feelings Chart* and point to how you feel when you think about this person or people.

Did the addicted person ever break any promises to you? If so, what promises did they break? How do you feel when promises are broken? I feel _____ towards _____ when they break their promises.

Has the person with an addiction caused damage or hurt to you or your family? If so, what ways are you hurt?
I feel ____towards _____ when they hurt me and my family.

Is there anything else you would like to share about knowing someone with an addiction?

Say To Yourself:

When someone I know has an addiction, I am allowed to feel all my good and not-so-good feelings. Addictions are complicated.

What Does Having an Addiction Mean?

It is not just Native people who suffer from addictions. People all over the world know someone who is addicted to alcohol, drugs, pills, or other substances. Addictions can happen to almost anyone, including young kids, teenagers, fathers, mothers, grandparents, aunts, uncles, cousins, friends, teachers, Elders, doctors, nurses, counsellors, coaches, and others.

People with addictions struggle and lose their way in life. Most want to quit, stay sober, and live a happy life.

When someone has an addiction, it means:

1. The person is drinking too much alcohol or using too many harmful drugs, pills, or other substances. The addicted person usually has problems at work, at home, or when alone because of their addiction.

2. Having an addiction also means the addicted person has a tough time stopping themselves from drinking or using harmful things once they start.

3. When an addicted person stops using alcohol or harmful substances, their body and mind usually start craving more of what they used. *Cravings* happen when the addicted person wants more, and their body needs more alcohol, drugs, pills, or other substances.

   For example, a person's body can get sick when they stop drinking alcohol or using drugs. The sickness is caused by the harmful things they use. This sickness will go away once the person stays sober long enough. However, instead of staying sober, some people keep drinking or using more. They do so to try and stop feeling sick. Using more harmful things to stop sickness only causes more problems later.

4. For some people, being lost in addiction also means they lose connection to their Spirit. When their Spirit feels far away, the addicted person drinks or uses again because they feel too lonely, too heart broken, lost, empty, and sad.

How Addictions Keep Happening

Alcohol, drugs, pills, and other substances are super powerful and dangerous. These harmful things act like the person's *Addiction Boss*. The Addiction Boss controls people's minds and bodies. These toxic substances also make the person feel drunk, relaxed, high, numb, or happy only for a while. These feelings go away once the alcohol, drugs, or pills wear off.

When the drunk or high feelings go away, the addicted person starts wanting more alcohol or dangerous drugs or pills. That is, their body and mind crave them. The addicted person starts feeling sick, bored, lonely, or sad and gives in to the cravings.

The Addiction Boss tells them to start using. The addicted person listens to the Addiction Boss because they feel vulnerable (weak), and they start drinking or *using* all over again. Soon, the addicted person feels trapped in *the cycle of addiction*. The picture on the opposite page shows how this addiction cycle keeps happening.

It is <u>so important</u> to know that young kids and teenagers can also get addicted very quickly. Using certain drugs *just one time* can cause addictions. These drugs move extremely fast to kids' brains and bodies and take over their lives. Before kids realize it, they can get trapped in the addiction cycle with an Addiction Boss.

Why Some Native People Use Addictive Substances in the First Place

Over the following pages, I will explain why some Native people *start* using alcohol, harmful drugs, pills, and other substances. Remember, there are many reasons besides the ones I discuss in this section.

World Problems and Native People

Many world problems cause great harm to Native people. Some people use alcohol and drugs to try and stop the pain these world problems cause. Even though many bad things happened before you or your parents were born, the problems did not go away. *The damage from long ago keeps hurting Native people today.* For example, racism hurts people and stops them from living the way Creator intended. The picture on the following page shows how racism harms many Native people.

Reasons Why Some Native People Hurt and Use Alcohol and DRUGS

Some non-Native people bully and lie to Native people. They take Native land, and they take their children.

Racism hurts Native people and stops many from getting a good education, and finding work to pay their bills.

World problems happened before you or your parents were born. These big problems keep damaging Native people and their families today.

Racism makes some Native people feel bad about themselves, and they feel ashamed of their Native culture.

Some people believe they are better than Native people, and they say mean things about them. Many non-Native people make fun of Native people, and this leads to great pain.

By: Geri Paul ©

World Problems Cause Damage

Racism

Racism is a big problem for Native people. *Racism* occurs when people believe they are better than Native people. Many people today are racists.

Racist people think they have the right to take Native people's land, control their lives, and treat them in horrible ways. Such beliefs and actions are wrong. Too many people end up living with painful and horrible consequences because of racism.

For example, too many people lose their way in life and turn to alcohol, drugs, and other substances to try and stop their pain. **However, using alcohol and drugs never heal people.** Abuse of alcohol and drugs always leads to even more hurt and damage. It is not the answer.

Native people must work extra hard with Creator and others to fight their addictions. World problems are too big for people to face alone.

On the next page are more reasons why some Native people start using alcohol, drugs, pills, and other substances.

Remember, using certain drugs, just one time, can cause a fast and dangerous addiction. Some drugs cause death, after using a small amount, just one time.

Also, remember, using too much alcohol, just one time, can cause an overdose and death. People can die from alcohol poisoning by drinking too much beer, vodka, whiskey, coolers, home brew, and any substance with alcohol.

On the next page, I talk about things that can happen when a person uses too much alcohol, drugs, pills, and other harmful substances.

Things that Can Happen When People Use Too Much Alcohol, Drugs, Pills, and Other Substances

People can feel lost, alone, and depressed; they feel their Spirit move away.

A person's body can get very sick, and brain damage can happen.

People die from overdoses or from other sicknesses caused by drugs and alcohol.

Others cannot control their behaviours and act dangerously. They drink and drive and can kill innocent people.

People can have anger outbursts. They can abuse and neglect their kids, others, themselves, and animals.

People lose their jobs or quit school.

Fighting, scaring people, and saying hurtful things also happens.

Many destroy property, lie, and steal things and money.

Some people get into trouble with the law, and sometimes end up in prison.

People spend all their money on addictions and cannot pay bills or buy food.

They are unable to provide a safe and healthy home for their children.

Many people stay stuck in their addictions and sadness. They lose hope.

Most parents and family members with addictions love their children very much. They do not want to hurt them. However, when people abuse alcohol, drugs, pills, or other harmful substances, their behaviours can spiral out of control. These unhealthy and often dangerous behaviours can cause terrible hurt and damage.

Remember, people with addictions are responsible for their behaviour. You did not cause the addicted person's harmful actions.

Also, remember, you are not responsible for solving adult problems. You cannot fix a person with an addiction. The addicted person needs to ask for help from other adults.

Help for People With Addictions
It is NEVER Too Late to Quit

Even though most people with addictions want to live a sober life, they need help doing so. It is up to the addicted person to ask for, and accept help.

The good news is, there is a lot of great support available for people with addictions. For example, Creator and Elders are always ready to help. Many professionals who work in addictions are also available. As well, there are special places people go to get healing.

- **Creator and Elders** - visiting Native Elders and attending ceremonies (or church) is important to healing. Creator loves everyone and takes pity on people who suffer with addictions.

- **Professional Help** - many professionals help people with addictions. Professional people include doctors, nurses, social workers, psychologists, psychiatrists, and addiction counsellors.

- **Special Places for Addictions** - people with addictions can also go to special places for healing. These places include rehabilitation centres (Rehab), detoxification centres (Detox), transition homes for sober living, and special in-person or online support groups are available.

Staying Away from Alcohol, Drugs, Marijuana, Pills, and Other Substances

Young children and teenagers can also get addicted to addictive substances. Should someone offer you these things, say no because they are extremely dangerous. *Marijuana also causes big problems because you can get addicted to it (weed, grass, dope, cannabis, and pot are other names for marijuana).*

Sometimes unhealthy adults ask kids to use drugs, drink alcohol, take pills, or smoke marijuana with them. *This is wrong.* You are allowed to say **NO** to adults. Say no to anyone who asks you to drink alcohol or use, including your parents, friends, and family.

Say To Yourself:

It is never OK for kids or teenagers to use alcohol or drugs. Even if an adult or my family says it is OK, I will still say "No" to using.

Things to Remember About Addictions

- ☐ If someone you know has an addiction, it is never your fault.

- ☐ You are a lovable kid who deserves to live in a safe home. You deserve to live in a home where people are not abusing alcohol, drugs, pills, or other things.

- ☐ It is not your job to fix people with addictions.

- ☐ Never take drugs, pills, alcohol, marijuana, or other substances. If the person asking is an adult or a family member, you must still <u>say no</u>.

- ☐ Young kids and teenagers can also get addicted very quickly.

- ☐ Kids and teenagers can die from alcohol poisoning, by using just one time.

Things to Remember About Addictions

- ☐ Kids can also overdose and die from taking a tiny bit of drugs or a small piece of a pill.

- ☐ Most people with addictions love their children very much; they want to stop *using* and live sober lives.

- ☐ People with addictions need help because most often they cannot stop on their own.

- ☐ Drugs, alcohol, pills, and other substances **NEVER** make pain disappear. It makes things worse.

- ☐ Feeling disappointed and upset at a person with an addiction is normal. Feeling upset does not make you a bad kid.

- ☐ Creator loves everyone, and he wants to help people with addictions. He also wants to help everyone hurting, including you and your family. If you are hurting, never stop asking for help.

Things People Get Addicted To

In the following pages, I explain several substances adults, teenagers, and kids can get addicted to. There are other addictive and dangerous substances besides the ones I list here. Also, people use many different names for the same drugs or pills. I am only using a few names in this book.

People can get addicted to the following:

- ☐ Alcohol
- ☐ Pain pills – opioids
- ☐ Other medicine from the doctor
- ☐ Street drugs from drug dealers, friends, family, and other people
- ☐ Other substances
- ☐ Marijuana (also called cannabis, weed, seed, grass, pot, or dope)

I will discuss each of these over the following few pages.

Alcohol - includes beer, wine, vodka, whiskey, rum, coolers, brandy, port, gin, tequila, champagne, sherry, ale, and homemade alcohol. Homemade alcohol is known as homebrew or moonshine. People can overdose and die from alcohol poisoning; by using it just one time.

Other substances containing alcohol include rubbing alcohol, mouthwash, and hand sanitizer. Aftershave, perfume, cologne, cough syrup, and flavoured extracts for cooking (like vanilla and almond flavouring) also contain alcohol.

 These other substances are extremely dangerous and should never be used to get drunk. They can poison people and lead to their death very quickly.

Pain Pills - include pills people get from the doctor for pain. Sometimes people ignore the doctor's instructions on how to take these pills. They use them to get high or to feel relaxed or numb. Taking pain pills safely and listening to the doctor's instructions are super important. Abusing certain pain pills leads to addictions, in some cases, death.

Opioids

Opioids are certain kinds of pain pills doctors prescribe. *Opioids* are also called *narcotics*. These medications are powerful and very addictive. Doctors prescribe these pills when people have really bad pain from surgery, dental work, headaches, and back pain. People also take opioids for many other injuries and pain. People can get tricked into believing their problems are better when they take these pills for too long.

Using too many opioids for a long time, can lead to addiction, overdose, and even death. It is hard to stop taking opioids once a person becomes addicted. Some people mix dangerous chemicals with opioids and sell them. This is wrong and against the law.

Never take any pills friends or drug dealers offer you. You can overdose with just a tiny amount after using it just one time.

Some Opioids Include:

- **Fentanyl**

- **Carfentanil** - should be used for giant animals only; it is not for people

- **Methadone**

- **Oxycodone** (for example, Oxycontin, Percocet, Percodan)

- **Hydrocodone**

- **Morphine** (for example, Heroin)

- **Codeine** (for example, Tylenol from the doctor)

- **Hydromorphone** (for example, Dilaudid, Exalgo)

- **Oxymorphone** (for example, Opana)

- **Tramadol** (for example, Ultram)

NALOXONE - NARCAN KIT

It is also essential you know about **NALOXONE**. Sometimes people use the word **NARCAN** instead of **NALOXONE**. Both terms refer to the same thing. Narcan is the *brand name* given to naloxone when it first came out.

Naloxone is used to help someone breathe when they overdose (OD) on opioids. A person overdoses and stops breathing when they take too many opioids, or they take a tiny amount of one pill. A naloxone kit nearby can save a person's life; it can help them breathe until they arrive at the hospital.

Naloxone kits come in a spray and is sprayed in a person's nose. Other kits come with a needle. Adults need to administer naloxone because it is not meant for kids to use on someone.

Other Medicine From the Doctors - Adults, teenagers, and kids can also get addicted to medicines besides opioids. Some people abuse other medications doctors prescribe.

Medicine given by the doctor is meant to help people with pain, anxiety, sadness, and sleeping problems. Some other people take prescribed medication because they feel too hyper and cannot focus very well. The doctor's instructions need to always be followed when taking any medications.

People can abuse medicine from the doctor to get high, to feel relaxed or numb, and to get extra energy. Some people also sell these medicines and mix them with other dangerous chemicals. When people misuse medication prescribed by the doctor, they can become addicted and overdose. People can also die when they do not follow the doctor's instructions.

A Few Medicines From the Doctor People Can Get Addicted To

- ☐ **Benzodiazepines** - used for anxiety and sleeping — slows the brain down (for example, Clonazepam, Diazepam).

- ☐ **Barbiturates** - used for sleeping and seizures - also slows the brain down (for example, Phenobarbital).

- ☐ **Stimulants** - used for being too hyper (for example, ADHD) and depression — makes the brain work faster (for example, Adderall, Vyvanse, Ritalin, Concerta).

- ☐ **Muscle Relaxers** — used for body pain (for example, Carisoprodol).

- ☐ **Sleep Medicine** — used to help people sleep (for example, Eszopiclone and Zaleplon).

- ☐ **Weight Loss Medicine** — used to help people lose weight (for example, Adipex-P and Didrex).

Drugs and Pills People Sell - People can get addicted to drugs and pills they buy or get for free from family, friends, strangers, and drug dealers. Drug dealers break the law and sell drugs and pills. They even sell pills prescribed by a doctor. Anyone selling these pills is breaking the law.

Some "street drugs and pills" are made secretly and contain very harmful ingredients. These dangerous ingredients can cause a very fast death. Methamphetamine (Meth) and crack cocaine are two examples of hazardous drugs people sell illegally.

Remember, never take any pills or drugs that friends, or drug dealers offer you. You can overdose with just a tiny amount, after using only one time.

A Few Drugs and Pills People Who Break the Law Sell

- ☐ **Opioids** — those from the doctor and those made secretly and "sold on the street."

    - ○ Fentanyl

- ☐ Methamphetamine (Meth)

- ☐ Cocaine

- ☐ Crack Cocaine

- ☐ Magic Mushrooms

- ☐ Marijuana

- ☐ Heroin

- ☐ **Other medications** - prescribed by a doctor like the ones I mentioned already.

Huffing and Other Substances - People can get high by sniffing and breathing in products containing harmful chemicals. This is called huffing and is very dangerous. Products people huff include hairspray, spray deodorant, gasoline, glue, paint thinner, and many other harmful things. Such products should never be used to get high. These substances are very addictive and dangerous. They cause a lot of damage to people's brains and bodies.

Some people also drink hazardous products containing alcohol like rubbing alcohol, mouth wash, and hand sanitizer. People also take aftershave, perfume, cologne, cough syrup, and flavoured extracts for cooking (like vanilla and almond flavouring). These dangerous substances should never be used to get drunk. They can cause poisoning and quickly lead to death.

Marijuana and Medicinal Marijuana

People can easily get fooled and believe marijuana is not addictive. Adults, teenagers, and kids can get addicted to marijuana and medicinal marijuana. People who use marijuana can have a tough time quitting. This drug is also called a *gateway drug* because it can lead people to use other harmful drugs and pills later.

People who sell marijuana can also lace it with other dangerous drugs and chemicals. Lacing means adding things to marijuana (like spraying it with Lysol — a cleaning product and adding opioids). Marijuana is also called cannabis, weed, pot, grass, or dope.

- ☐ Creator did not give us the marijuana plant to abuse in unhealthy ways.

- ☐ Marijuana is addictive and it can hurt people.

- ☐ Children, teenagers, and young adults should not use marijuana because it negatively affects their brain growth and development.

Medicinal marijuana is used to help people when they have health problems; it is prescribed by doctors. Doctors may do so when people have long-term pain, cancer, severe mental health concerns, and seizures. Doctors also prescribe medicinal marijuana for other health concerns such as long-term tummy issues (for example, when people cannot stop throwing up).

Some people also abuse medicinal marijuana and do not use it as the doctor intended. Medicinal marijuana should not be shared or sold to other people. It is addictive and can hurt people, and it should only be used like the doctor prescribed.

People Use Marijuana in Many Ways

A Few Ways Include:

- ☐ **Smoking it** with a pipe, a bong, or a joint.
- ☐ **Eating it** - people eat things like marijuana brownies and gummy candy. They also chew marijuana leaves.
- ☐ **Mixing it** in water or a drink like tea. This marijuana comes in powder.
- ☐ **Rubbing it on the skin** - this marijuana comes in a lotion or a gel.
- ☐ **Applying a patch** — a marijuana patch is put on a person's skin.
- ☐ **Using marijuana drops** — people put marijuana drops under their tongues.
- ☐ **Swallowing it** — people swallow marijuana pills.

Next, I will move to Chapter 8 and talk about another important topic, "When Someone You Know Passes Away." If you are not ready to read about death, you can skip the next chapter and read it later.

CHAPTER 8

When Someone You Know Passes Away

Many feelings and thoughts happen when someone passes away. In this chapter, I talk about feelings and experiences you may have if you know someone who died. Talking about death can be difficult. Make sure you sit with an adult you trust when reading this chapter. If you feel too overwhelmed, you can skip this section and return later. If you feel OK, please read the following six points before moving forward.

Six Points to Read Before Continuing

1. **Ask an adult you trust and feel comfortable with, to read this chapter with you.** You can have the adult sit near you while you read, or the adult can read to you. You can also take turns reading.

2. **Do not rush reading.** Read a little at a time if this feels best. You may take all the time you need to remember the person who passed away.

3. **Take breaks from reading** and give yourself some quiet time to feel and cry if you need to. Crying is healing and a healthy and normal thing to do.

4. **Ask an adult about anything you do not understand or remember.** All your questions are important.

5. If you feel overwhelmed and anxious, **practice the deep belly breathing exercise in Chapter 6.** You may take a breather any time. I also include the exercise again, on the following page, so you can practice your deep breathing right now.

6. **If you need extra help and are feeling stuck since your loss, ask an adult to find an Elder or another professional to help you.** Remember, many people need help when someone passes away. You do not have to grieve alone!

Deep Breathing Exercise

1. Breathe in good thoughts through your nose, deep in your tummy, all the way to your belly button. Count to five as you breathe in.

2. Hold your breath by your belly button, and count to three.

3. Now, breathe out bad enery and bad thoughts very slowly, through your mouth. Count to five as you breathe out.

4. Say to yourself, "I did a good job. I will be OK."

5. Repeat the steps above four more times.

This chapter is broken down into the following three parts.

Part 1

- Grieving
- What does passing away mean?
- The wake and the funeral

Part 2

- Remembering the person who passed away, and *a memory relationship*
- Understanding *why* people pass away

Part 3

- Feelings and taking care of yourself
- Taking breaks from grieving
- In summary, things to remember when someone passes away

Part 1

- Grieving
- What does passing away mean?
- The wake and the funeral

Grieving

When someone passes away, *grieving* and *mourning* are normal and natural things to do. Grieving means letting yourself remember and feel all your feelings. Mourning includes talking about the person and doing things to remember and honour them. Even though grieving and mourning are painful and often upsetting, <u>you must do it</u>. If you ignore your feelings and thoughts for too long, you could feel much worse later.

Do not *stay stuck* in unhealthy ways of grieving. On the next page is an example of an erupting grief volcano. This volcano shows what could happen when someone tries to stop their grieving and mourning. People can become stuck, and they keep hurting and suffering.

Unhealthy Grief Volcano

If You Do Not Grieve In Healthy Ways, Grief Feelings Sometimes Erupt In Hurtful Behaviours

- Worrying Other People Will Die
- Unable to Sleep or Eat
- Afraid to Be Alone
- Yelling
- Feeling Sick
- Disobeying Rules
- Hitting
- Biting
- Breaking Things
- Throwing
- Spitting
- Hurting Yourself
- Stop Praying
- Scared to Leave Your Parents

Hurt

Sad

Scared

Lonely

Confused

Feeling Guilty

Frustrated

Mad

Angry

By: Geri Paul ©

If you feel stuck in grief or you are erupting in hurtful ways, talk to an adult you trust and let them help you. I will provide examples of how you can ask for help later in this chapter.

Say To Yourself:
I am allowed to grieve and remember the person who passed away. I can also ask for help when I feel sad and confused about my thoughts and feelings.

Everyone Grieves Differently

Everyone grieves and mourns in different ways. For example, some people may talk a lot about the person who passed away; others talk very little. Some people may also smile and share happy memories. Other people may smile very little and not share any memories at all.

Also, everyone heals differently and returns to normal activities at different times. For example, some people may feel ready to go back to school, work, or join sports soon after the passing. Other people may take longer to return to life activities.

There is no *one* way to grieve, and there is no need to try and finish your grieving too soon. Everyone grieves in their own way, including you. Try to not compare yourself to how other people are doing. Your walk with grief will be different than other people's walks. That is perfectly OK.

In the next section, I talk about what passing away means. I also discuss what might happen to a person's Spirit when they leave their *earth body*.

What Does Passing Away Mean?

When someone *passes away*, they stop breathing and will not wake up again. The person stopped living in their **earth body**. Earth body is the body you were born with. It is the body you see when you look in the mirror.

Also, as you probably know, when someone passes away, their body gets buried or cremated. *Cremated* means the person's body is put in a particular place at a funeral home and burned into ashes. The family decides where to put the ashes and where to bury the person. The person's Spirit has already left their body, so they do not feel hurt from being buried or cremated.

Where Does Someone's Spirit Go When They Leave Their Earth Body?

Our Spirit lives inside our body, our mind, and our heart. Spirit is all around. When someone dies, many people believe their Spirit keeps living.

They believe the person's Spirit goes to heaven or the *Spirit World* with Creator and other people who passed away.

Some people also feel the person's Spirit stays on earth for a while before it *crosses over* to heaven or the Spirit world. Other people think that when someone passes away, their Spirit returns to earth and lives in an animal or a *different* human body.

Every Native tribe and family have their own beliefs about what happens to someone's Spirit in the afterlife. If you have more questions about the afterlife, the best people to talk with are the adults in your own Native family.

> Remember, all your questions are important. Never stop asking and learning.

The Wake and Funeral

Every Native tribe and family have their own ways of caring for their loved one's body and Spirit. There are many important customs and rituals to help families do this. These customs and rituals are unique and happened long before Europeans and other people came to North America.

Following *customs* and *rituals* means caring for the person who passed away in special and respectful ways. For example, there are rules to follow and meaningful ways of doing things at the wake, the funeral, and during other ceremonies. I only talk a little about the wake and funeral here.

The Wake

The *wake* follows many customs and rituals. During the wake, family and friends are given a chance to visit the person's body and pay their respects. The person's Spirit is honoured, and other ceremonies also take place. In some tribes, the wake lasts four days, and a smudge burns the whole time. Special Native songs are sung at some wakes. It is also customary for someone to stay with the body for the entire four days. The person's body is also dressed and prepared in particular ways. The family usually does this before the wake starts. You can ask your Native family about other important customs which I do not cover in this book.

The Funeral

After the wake, **a funeral** happens. A *funeral* is a ceremony that also has special customs and rituals. The funeral usually lasts a few hours or half a day. Family, friends, and community members gather around the body one last time. A service or a ceremony happens at the funeral, and people pray, sing, and a few people will give a speech and talk about the person who passed away. The service or ceremony can occur in a church, a funeral home, or other places. Some people believe that singing and praying help the person's Spirit travel home to the Spirit world.

Once the service or ceremony ends, the person's body is brought to a final resting place and put in a grave. The resting place can be a special place on the land, such as the family property or somewhere else in nature. The grave can also be in a cemetery. If the person was cremated, the resting place could be on land, in a graveyard, or some other place like the mountains or the ocean.

> **Say To Yourself:**
> Learning my family's customs and rituals when someone passes away is important. Understanding this is part of my healthy grieving.

Before we move to Part 2, ensure you check in with the adult reading with you. Reading this chapter can be upsetting and painful for many kids. So, checking in regularly and taking breaks are necessary.

The adult can check and ask the following questions.

- How are you feeling?

- Is there anything else you need to talk about before we continue reading?

- Do you have any questions?

- Do you need to take a break, stretch, drink some water, or deep breathe?

Part 2

- Remembering the person who passed away, and *a memory relationship*
- Understanding why people pass away

Remembering the Person Who Passed Away and a Memory Relationship

As I mentioned, every Native tribe and family have their own ways of honouring people who pass away. A few examples include having *feasts, Spiritual ceremonies,* "*specials*", and *giveaways*.

- **Feasts** - some Native people have feasts to remember and honour their loved ones. Some feasts are for family and friends. Other feasts are much larger and can include entire communities. During these gatherings, a lot of good food is prepared and shared. Sometimes a particular food offering is given to Creator and the grandfathers and grandmothers. Some people also feed their loved one's Spirit.

- **Spiritual Ceremonies** and **"Specials"** - families also honour and remember their loved ones by having Spiritual ceremonies where Elders help with prayers. As well, some families will have "specials" as a way of honouring their loved one. For example, during one type of "special", prize money or gifts are given to people who win singing and dancing contests at pow-wows.

- **Giveaways** - other families have giveaways where presents are given to the public. Giveaways can happen at pow-wows, ceremonies, or wherever the family chooses.

A Memory Relationship

Remembering people who passed away is very important. Some kids and adults, too, worry they might forget their loved one. For example, they feel nervous and scared if they are not thinking about their loved one enough. This seems to happen when people smile more and start doing fun things again.

Remember, feeling happiness again does not mean forgetting about your loved one. It is **OK** to smile again. You are allowed to remember your loved one and still do your favourite things. For example, you can have belly laughs, ride your bike or skateboard, watch your favourite **TV** shows, go to a movie, or spend time with your friends.

> You will not forget about your loved one because you have a *memory relationship* with them.

Having a *memory relationship* means your connection to your loved one keeps happening. The person's memory is still in your mind, heart, and Spirit. Of course, the new relationship is different from when the person was alive. Even though you cannot see the person, hear them, feel their hugs, or talk to them like you used to, you still have an ongoing memory relationship.

Having a *memory relationship* with the person who passed away means:

- You hold a special place in your heart just for them.

- You think about the person and still talk to them in your mind or out loud.

- You want to keep remembering many things about them.

- And you *do* something to remember and honour them.

Most memory relationships happen naturally on their own. You do not need to rush and worry about creating new ways of remembering your loved one too quickly.

If you choose not to continue a memory relationship with someone, that is perfectly OK, too. Making this decision does not mean you are a bad kid. I am sure you have good reasons for your choice.

Some of these reasons might include any of the following:

- You do not feel ready for a memory relationship.

- You do not feel close to the person who passed away.

- The person who passed away was not nice. They were not kind to you, or they hurt you.

- The person who passed away caused hurt or damage to other people.

Suppose you decide to add to a memory relationship; in that case, I outline a few ways you can do this over the following pages.

Talking About the Person Who Passed Away

People in some Native tribes do not talk about the person who passed away, or look at their photos or videos, until some time passes. For example, some people wait one full year since the death before they speak about their loved one. Every Native tribe has unique grieving traditions. Learn about and follow your family's customs around grieving.

When it is traditionally appropriate, talking about the person who passed away is an important part of grieving. Sharing your thoughts and feelings with someone you trust also adds to your *memory relationship*. Sharing makes your relationship stronger.

Tears and laughter are healing

When you talk about the person who passed away, you may feel like crying or laughing or doing both. Do not try and hold these feelings back. Your tears and laughter are necessary ways of honouring and remembering your relationship.

Adults also cry and need to let their feelings happen. If you see an adult crying in front of you, this is **OK**. You do not need to try and stop or fix the adult's feelings. I will talk much more about feelings a little later.

For now, let us begin talking more about the people you know who passed away. If there is something you do not know, ask the adult with you. Start by answering these questions.

> **Who are the people you know who passed away?**
> - You can write the people's names down or say their names out loud.
> - You can also remember them in your mind.
> - Or, you can point to the circles on the next page.

Can you share a little about the people who passed away?
- How do you know them? Are you related?
- What did they look like?
- How old were they when they passed away?
- Do you know how or why they passed away?

Time To Check-In

I already mentioned that reading this chapter can be upsetting and painful for many kids. So, it is important for the adult reader to check in with you before continuing.

 The adult can check and ask the following questions.

- How are you feeling?

- Is there anything else you need to talk about before we continue reading?

- Do you have any questions?

- Do you need to take a break, stretch, drink some water, or deep breathe?

How to Make A Memory Book

Let us continue and learn about making a memory book. Making a memory book is another way you can add to your memory relationship. Your book can be dedicated to the person who passed away, or it can be a gift to yourself or someone else. You can visit your book as often as you like. Below are a few points on how to make a memory book.

- You can use any paper (construction paper, coloured paper, lined or unlined paper, or fancy paper).

- You can use any book (a photo book, binder, diary, or notebook). Some people also make their memory book on the computer using PowerPoint.

- You can include as many people as you like.

- You can also add anything you want in your book.

Here are a few examples of what to include in your memory book.

You can include photos, poems, dried flowers, artwork, feathers, songs, or beaded things. Also, try writing a letter to or drawing a picture of the person who passed away. You can add almost anything you want. You can also keep adding new things whenever you like. Your memory book can keep growing; add items for as long as you wish. For example, in my memory book, I included many notes and letters.

Below is an example of a note I wrote when I was really missing my grandfather.

To My Grandfather

Dear Poppy,

The day you died, my heart broke and I sat on my bed alone and cried. I felt angry because you left me. I still miss you, and I cry for you, but I am not so mad anymore. I wish I could see you and talk, just one more time. I miss your singing. I love you Poppy, and I will write to you again soon. XOXO Geri

Add A Favourite Story

Also, consider including a favourite story in your memory book.

- You can write, draw, or create a song or a video about your story.

- Your story can include anything. For example, it can be a funny or sad memory.

- Perhaps you can share a story about doing something together like walking, fishing, watching **TV**, cooking, beading, hunting, or shopping.

Extra Information to Include in Your Story

You can include more information in your story by answering the following questions. Ask an adult to help if there is information you do not know. You may even find yourself learning new and exciting things about the person who passed away. Some questions include:

- Where did they grow up?

- Where did they work? Where did they attend school?

- What was their favourite food?

- What Native events or ceremonies did they attend?

- What was their favourite sport, movie, or hobby?

- What was their personality like? Were they funny, shy, serious, super talkative, a little grumpy at times, or quiet?

On the following page is an example of a story I included in my memory book.

Memory Book

One of My Favourite Memories

My grandfather is my favourite person. He never went to school because he grew up hunting, fishing, and building boats. He talked quietly and loved telling stories of the old days and his hunting trips. He also loved to sing and dance. We had so much fun together. I always felt my grandfather's love.

One of my favourite memories is the day we pulled the trap full of cod fish. There were so many fish they almost went over the boat's sides. The whole family worked extremely hard, putting all the fish away. We laughed and shared stories until dark. The next morning, my grandmother fried one of those fish for breakfast. My grandmother always fried my fish just right. I also loved eating her homemade bread and drinking hot tea. I miss those days with my grandparents very much.

Next, I will move on and discuss a few reasons why people pass away. This section can also be very upsetting for many kids. I want to remind the adult reader to continue doing regular check-ins throughout this chapter. The adult can check and ask you the questions we previously reviewed. These include the following:

- How are you feeling?

- Is there anything else you need to talk about before we continue reading?

- Do you have any questions?

- Do you need to take a break, stretch, drink some water, or deep breathe?

Understanding Why People Pass Away

An important part of your grieving is understanding what caused the person to die. Some reasons people pass away include the following.

Accidents

Old Age

Sicknesses

Babies can pass away before or soon after birth

Suicide

Murder

Unknown Reasons

Old Age and Babies

Some people pass away because they are elderly. They reach old age and die *a natural* death; their bodies wear out and stop working so well. Older people can also die from sicknesses that come with aging.

Babies pass away for different reasons. Some babies die from health problems, accidents, and being born prematurely (before their body grows big enough). Babies can also have diseases or weak little organs when they are born (like weak hearts, lungs, kidneys, or livers). Other babies pass away while still inside their mothers' tummies.

Sicknesses

People also pass away from sicknesses. Some of these sicknesses include:

- Cancer, coronavirus (COVID), heart attacks, diabetes, and other diseases they were born with or developed later.

- Strokes (blood clots in the brain), brain tumours (lumps in the brain), brain diseases (like Alzheimer's disease and dementia), bone diseases, and multiple sclerosis (MS).

- Liver disease (like cirrhosis, fatty liver), lung sickness (like pneumonia), HIV/AIDS, kidney disease, sickness related to addictions, and other blood sicknesses (like leukemia).

Sudden Unexpected Deaths

A sudden unexpected death happens when someone passes away very fast without any warning. This type of death is shocking and can feel like it is not real. It may seem like you are watching a bad movie, or you are in a terrible dream. Some people say they are waiting for this bad movie or dream to end so they can see the person who died again.

When death happens unexpectedly, it is normal to feel shocked, numb, and like the event is unreal. Sudden and unexpected deaths include passing away from the following:

- Sicknesses like the ones we have already talked about
- A broken heart
- Accidents
- Accidental overdose
- Murder/homicide
- Unknown reasons
- Suicide

A broken heart — passing away from a broken heart usually happens when someone feels sad for too long and cannot find any more happiness. A person can sometimes feel so sad their heart breaks, and they pass away. Other times, a person's body and heart take on too much sadness and stress. They can become sick and pass away suddenly.

Accidents — accidents happen in many ways. Accidents occur while driving vehicles like cars, trucks, snowmobiles, four wheelers, boats, motorcycles, airplanes, and bicycles. Some accidents also happen while using farming equipment. Other times vehicles hit people and they pass away.

Accidents also include getting hit by lightning or ending up in a house fire. People can accidently drown, choke, get lost in the woods, freeze from the outdoors, and get attacked by animals (like bears, cougars, or dogs). If people do not eat enough food or drink enough water, or if they eat something poisonous, they can accidently die. Injuries from work, skateboarding, riding a scooter, from playing sports, and slipping or falling also cause deaths.

Accidental overdose — people can accidentally overdose and pass away from taking too many pills or harmful drugs. Accidental overdose also includes drinking too much alcohol (alcohol poisoning) and taking other dangerous substances. Even taking a little bit of dangerous drugs, pills, or substances could cause an overdose. People can also overdose and pass away from using just once.

Murder/homicide — when a person passes away from a murder/homicide, it means another person took their life. The person who takes another person's life can be a stranger or someone the person knows. You may have already heard about the many missing and murdered Indigenous people. As well, there are many children's graves being discovered near old residential school land. I will talk much more about residential schools in Chapter 10.

Unknown reasons — people can sometimes pass away for reasons we do not understand. For example, people can die in their sleep or not wake up from surgery. No one can explain what caused their hearts to stop beating. Even doctors cannot always tell why some people pass away. You do not need to worry about passing away in your sleep because this is very rare and very unlikely to happen to people.

Suicide

When a person *dies by suicide*, it means they ended their own life. People take their own lives for many different reasons. No one knows for sure why someone died by suicide. However, a few reasons someone may take their own life include the following:

- The person was feeling very sad and alone.

- They felt hopeless and believed life would not get any better.

- Some people were bullied or abused and felt they could not take it anymore.

- The person was *not thinking clearly* and felt overwhelmed because of hurt and stress.

- The person was *not thinking clearly* because they took drugs or drank too much alcohol.

- The person thought suicide was OK because they knew other people who took their own lives. Remember, suicide is **NEVER OK**.

- They were thinking and feeling suicide is the **only** answer to their problems.

- The person was missing someone who passed away and believed they will see them again when they die.

- They were not feeling lovable.

- The person believed no one would miss them.

- They believed they were a burden to everyone.

- They also believed suicide is OK because a group of people decided to end their lives together.

- The person felt pressured to die by suicide because a friend or someone else said they will die together, as a couple, or as best friends.

Remember, suicide is never OK. It is not the answer. **If you feel like taking your own life, ALWAYS tell an adult immediately.** Never keep this a secret. You are a lovable kid, and you are not doing anything wrong by expressing how you feel. Here are two examples of what you can say if you feel suicidal:

- "I feel like taking my own life. I need help."

- "I do not feel well. I do not feel like living, and I need help."

You can also write or text your message if you feel uncomfortable talking about suicide.

 This is your check-in reminder. The adult reading with you should ask you the following questions.

- How are you feeling right now?

- Do you ever feel like taking your own life?

- Is there anything else you need to talk about before we continue reading?

- Do you have any questions?

- Do you need to take a break, stretch, drink some water, or deep breathe?

To the adult: if someone says they are suicidal, ensure you do not ignore this. Find professional help for your child.

Say To Yourself: I will tell an adult if I feel like taking my own life. People care about me, and I am not doing anything wrong by saying how I feel.

When Someone Tells You They Feel Suicidal

If someone says they want to take their own life, you **must** tell an adult. Even if the person made you promise to keep it secret, you must tell. If the person is an adult (like a parent or another relative), you must still share this with another adult. This is a time you must break a secret. You can also encourage the person who feels suicidal to tell an adult right away. Here is an example of what you can say:

"You can get help. You must tell an adult about this. And I must tell an adult, too."

You can also call *"The Kid's Help Line"*, a place where kids can text or call for help 24-7. You can get the number online or dial zero (0) and ask for it. Remember, you still need to tell an adult, too.

Here is an example of what you can say when you call for help: "My friend (or parent, or relative) is telling me they want to take their own life. They need help. What should I do?"

Some Things to Remember About Suicide

- Never keep suicide a secret.

- People who feel suicidal are not thinking clearly. They are probably hurting badly, overwhelmed, confused, drunk or high and need professional help.

- Telling an adult can save your life or another person's life.

- Never assume someone is joking or "looking for attention" when they talk about suicide.

- Even if someone gets mad at you for telling, that is OK. Saving someone's life and getting help are more important than worrying about keeping suicide a secret.

- Plus, when you tell, you are a good friend. Even if the person gets mad at you, that is OK.

- There is help for people who feel sad, hopeless, and suicidal. Never stop asking for help!

If the adult you tell does not find help immediately, keep telling other people.

Adults You Can Talk to if You or Someone Feels Suicidal

- A parent, grandparent, auntie, uncle, adult cousin, adult sibling, or a trusted family friend.

- An Elder, a doctor, a nurse, a teacher, a social worker, a police officer, a counsellor, a minister, a coach, a friend's mother or father, or a trusted neighbour.

- You can also talk to someone at The Kid's Help Line or call 911. Here is their contact information again.

Call or text **The Kid's Help Line 24-7.** Look online for the number or call Zero (0) and ask. Here is an example of what you can say:

"I am a kid, and I need The Kid's Helpline number, please."

Call 911 if you cannot reach the helpline and tell them you or someone else is feeling suicidal.

Call 911 Right Away If Any of the Following Happens

- You tried to take your own life by taking pills or any other dangerous substance. Call 911.

- You tried to take your own life by cutting yourself, hanging yourself, or doing something dangerous. Call 911.

- You are thinking about or planning on taking your own life. Call 911.

- If someone says they plan on taking their life or have attempted suicide already. For example, if they tell you they took pills, cut themselves or plan to die. Call 911.

Remember, you are **not** a bad kid and are not doing anything wrong by asking for help. Reaching out means you are being your own good friend or a good friend to someone else. You deserve support because you are a lovable kid! Also, try to remember that many people want to help kids who are hurting, feeling hopeless, and confused.

> **Say To Yourself:**
> Suicide is very serious. I will not ignore a person who says they want to kill themselves. I will tell an adult <u>right away</u> if this happens. I will also tell an adult immediately if I feel suicidal.

Should the adult you ask get angry, ignore you, or say you are OK, keep seeking help from other adults. Never stop reaching out. There are people who care about you.

Knowing Someone Who Died By Suicide

If you know someone who passed away by suicide, remember the following:

- It is not your fault. You did not cause the person to take their own life. Even if you were arguing when they passed away, it is still not your fault.

- Also, you could not stop this from happening. The person who passed away made the decision to die because they were struggling in different ways.

- You are allowed to have your feelings, thoughts, and questions about your loss.

- Talk to an adult you trust. Ask them to find extra help if you struggle with your loss or feel stuck.

- You are lovable, and you deserve help!

 This is your check-in reminder. The adult reading with you should ask you the following questions.

- How are you feeling right now?

- Is there anything else you need to talk about before we continue reading?

- Do you have any questions?

- Do you need to take a break, stretch, drink some water, or deep breathe?

Part 3

- Feelings and taking care of yourself
- Taking breaks from grieving
- Summary of things to remember

Feelings and Taking Care of Yourself

When someone passes away, taking good care of yourself is extremely important. One way to do this is by being your own good friend. Being your own good friend includes letting yourself grieve. You are allowed to let yourself have your "Good" and "Not-So-Good" feelings. The *Indigenous Feelings Chart* on the next page shows some feelings you may experience.

Say To Yourself: When someone passes away, it is normal to have good and not-so-good feelings. All my feelings are important.

Remember, all your feelings are gifts from Creator. Your feelings let you know what is happening inside of you.

Sorting Out Your Feelings

It is normal to have many different feelings when someone passes away. At times, these feelings may seem overwhelming and hard to figure out.

Feeling confused and having opposite feelings from time to time is also expected. For example, you might feel happy one minute and very sad the next. You may also feel relieved the person passed away, and at the same time, you may feel guilty for feeling relieved. All these feelings are normal.

It is also normal for kids to need help sorting through their mixture of feelings. The "Sorting Out Your Feelings Machine" on the next page can help you with this process. Just remember, you do not need to experience every feeling. Some feelings may never happen, and others may come through later. This is OK.

Below are examples of how you can start talking about, or writing down, your feelings. It is good to start your sentences with the words "I feel" and then complete your statement. Remember, everything you feel is correct. There are no incorrect feelings.

"I feel ____ when I think about laughing and having fun again."

"I feel ____ because I will not see ____ in their earth body again."

"I feel ____ when I think about ____ (name the person who passed away)."

"I feel ____ when I think about a happy memory we had together."
"When I think about a sad memory, I feel ____."

 This is your check-in reminder. The adult reading with you should ask you the following questions.

- How are you feeling right now?

- Is there anything else you need to talk about before we continue reading?

- Do you have any questions?

- Do you need to take a break, stretch, drink some water, or deep breathe?

Feeling Scared, Guilty, Numb, and Relieved When Someone Passes Away

In the following section, I will talk a little more about feeling *scared, guilty, numb,* and *relieved.*

Feeling scared is normal when someone passes away. Kids can feel scared for many reasons. For example, some children feel afraid and worry about what will happen since the person is no longer here. Other kids worry that they might die, or someone close to them might pass away, too. Remember, when someone passes away, it does not mean you or another person close to you will also die.

Feeling guilty is another normal feeling people can experience. Children can feel guilty for many reasons, including the following:

- Feeling guilty because they believe they could have done more and perhaps stopped the person from dying.

- Feeling guilty because they did not spend enough time with the person.

- Feeling guilty because they enjoy not having to visit or help take care of the person anymore.

- Feeling guilty because they fought and said mean words or ignored the person who passed away.

- Feeling guilty because they did not do what the person asked before they passed away.

- Feeling guilty for not being there when the person died.

Remember, you did not cause the person to pass away, and you could not have stopped it from happening. Also, it is normal to wish you could go back in time and change some things. Even though you cannot change the past, it is important to still talk to someone about the things you wish you did differently. Sharing is an important part of your healing and grieving.

Feeling numb — when children feel numb it means they do not experience all the feelings they would usually feel. Sometimes numbness can seem like you feel "nothing", "blank", "shock", or "dead inside." Also, when someone appears numb with a blank or non-caring look, it does not mean they do not care.

If you feel numb, this does not mean you are a bad kid. **Feeling numb for a while can be a good thing.** Numbness can help you survive the trauma and pain of losing someone.

The following are a few extra points about feeling numb.

- Numb feelings can help protect kids' hearts and bodies from getting overwhelmed by their hurt.

- The numbness puts upset feelings on hold so kids can continue doing everyday things like eating, sleeping, and showering.

- Often Native people feel numb because they already lost too many people. Too many Native people are passing away from suicide, accidents, sicknesses, and accidental drug overdoses.

- Many Native families also lose a lot of people in a very short time. Such loss is not normal. It is shocking and causes overwhelming feelings of grief and pain.

- Therefore, some people's heads, hearts, bodies, and Spirits are so full of hurt and sadness they need to feel numb for a while. Once the numbness wears off, the hurt and sadness appear again.

- The numb feelings act like a protection because it helps Native people from getting too overwhelmed and sick. In many cases, feeling numb allows people to continue surviving through their terrible losses.

- Numbness usually goes away when time passes.

> Remember, when people appear numb, this does not mean they do not care about the person who passed away. It also does not mean they do not care about other people's sad experiences. Feeling numb usually means the person's feelings are on hold for a while because the loss is too much to process right now.

Feeling relieved is another normal feeling kids can experience when someone passes away. Feeling relieved means feeling less heavy, less pressured, or less anxious since the person died. There are many reasons for feeling relieved including the following:

- Feeling relieved because you believe the person is no longer hurting or suffering with pain or sadness.

- You can feel relieved because you do not worry about *where* the person is living anymore and whether they are safe.

- Believing your loved one is with family and others in the Spirit world can also bring some kids a relief feeling.

- Knowing the person who passed away can no longer hurt you or anyone else is another reason kids feel relieved.

- As well, knowing you do not need to visit or help care for the person anymore can bring a sense of relief.

Remember, if you feel relieved, scared, guilty, or numb since losing someone, this does not mean you are a bad or terrible kid.

Other Experiences

In addition to experiencing all your feelings, many other things can happen when someone you know passes away. Over the following few pages, I will talk a little more about these *other experiences*. Remember, the topics we are about to discuss, do not happen for everyone. Some of these experiences include:

- Looking for the person who passed away

- Feeling the person around

- Having many up-and-down feelings and emotions

- Wanting to be alone

- Believing you will always feel this sad

- Crying

Looking for the person who passed away happens when someone expects to see them alive again. For example, seeing someone with the same hair colour, who dresses or walks the same way, who talks similarly, or is the same age causes some people to check. They look and see if it is the person who died. Others also find themselves waiting for the person to come home, call, text, or email. These behaviours are normal. No one knows exactly why this happens. If you find yourself looking or waiting to see the person again, a few guesses why this occurs include the following:

- You may still experience shock and do not believe the person passed away yet.

- Even though your mind knows the person died, your Spirit does not know.

- Maybe you miss your loved one so much, your Spirit keeps looking and hoping to see them alive again.

- You are not feeling ready to say goodbye.

Remember, looking for the person who died usually happens less as more time passes.

Feeling the person around, smelling or hearing them is also common for some people. Others also see the person in Spirit form or in their dreams. This can happen before or after the person dies.

Many up-and-down feelings, which change quickly, also happens. For example, one minute you may feel sad and start crying. The same minute, you may feel happy and start laughing. Feelings can sometimes change daily, from hour to hour or from minute to minute.

Wanting to be alone when someone passes away is very common for some people. Spending time alone is good because it gives you privacy to sort through your thoughts and feelings. However, do not spent too much time by yourself. Being around people who care about you is important for your grieving.

Believing you will always feel this sad is another natural feeling kids can experience. Losing someone you love can cause great sadness. Your heart, Spirit, mind, and body will probably go through a lot of hurt and pain. This pain may seem like it will never end. Try to remember such heavy sadness will *change* over time.

The waves of hurt, sadness, and loneliness will get further apart. The sadness will happen less often. In between the waves of pain and loneliness, you will have moments of feeling happy again. You are allowed to smile and feel joy. Smiling does not mean you forget the person who passed away.

Crying is also a normal thing to do when someone passes away. People shed their tears differently. For example, some people cry loudly while others do it very quietly. As well, some people only cry when they are alone. Others are OK showing their tears in front of people.

Further, some people burst into tears the moment anyone mentions the person who passed away. Other people do not cry right away. Instead, they wait until the wake and funeral are over, or when their life starts returning to normal again. Then their crying starts. It is also common for some people to wait and cry when their shock and numbness start to wear off.

More Ways People Cry When Someone Passes Away

- Some people feel like crying all the time.

- Others are scared to cry. They worry they may not stop once they have started.

- People can also feel guilty or like a bad person because they have not cried.

- Some people feel they are cried empty and cannot shed another tear.

- As well, other people can feel uncomfortable when someone sees them cry. So, they do not let their tears happen in front of others.

- People can feel they will not stop crying when they see other people's tears.

- Also, some people believe that crying is a sign of being a weak person.

- Finally, some people believe crying for too long will keep their loved one's Spirit on earth. They believe it is OK to cry, but to do so in balanced ways.

Things to Remember About Crying

- Your tears are gifts from Creator, and they help you heal.

- Whichever way you cry is OK. You are allowed to shed tears in your own way.

- If you try to stop crying, it can hurt you more later.

- You are allowed to let others show their tears in front of you, even if it makes you uncomfortable.

- You do not need to try and fix or stop other people from hurting or crying.

- Talk to someone if you are worried about how you cry. Sharing is good because it can help you understand your grief and healing.

Say To Yourself:

People cry differently. I am also allowed to cry in my own way when it feels OK to do so.

Taking Breaks From Grieving

Another way to practice being your own good friend is by letting yourself take breaks from grieving. Grieving is hard work; everyone needs time away every now and again. You are allowed to take breaks from remembering the person who passed away and play and laugh. A few self-care things you can do on your break include playing outside and laughing at funny movies or jokes. You can also play with or walk your pet, read a happy book, and spend time with your friends.

Say To Yourself:

I give myself permission to take breaks from thinking about the person who passed away. I am allowed to play and feel happy again.

Asking for Help When Someone Passes Away

Talk to an adult if you feel alone, sad, or confused. You do not have to carry your loss all alone. You are allowed to ask for support. You can also ask your parents or an adult to find an Elder or a professional person to talk to you. Here are two examples of how you can let someone know you need help:

- "I feel sad and lonely. I need help figuring out my feelings."

- "Can you find someone I can talk to? I am having trouble and need help since __ passed away."

You can also call The Kid's Helpline. They have kind and supportive people who want to hear you. The support line is available 24-7 (every day, at any time). The number for your area is online. You can dial zero, 0 and ask for **The Kid's Helpline** number as well.

 This is your check-in reminder. The adult reading with you should ask you the following questions.

- How are you feeling right now?

- Is there anything else you need to talk about before we continue reading?

- Do you have any questions?

- Do you need to take a break, stretch, drink some water, or deep breathe?

Things to Remember When Someone Passes Away

- It is normal to have many different feelings when someone passes away. It takes time to sort them out.

- People pass away for many reasons; it is never your fault. You could not stop the person from dying.

- You will not forget the person who passed away because you have a *memory relationship* with them.

- You must practice good self-care and become your own good friend. Letting yourself grieve, taking breaks to do enjoyable activities, and asking for help are three ways you can practice self-care.

- You are allowed to smile and enjoy some of your favourite things again.

I will now move to the next chapter. In Chapter 9, I discuss many more self-care ideas.

CHAPTER 9

Taking Care of Your Spirit: Your Body, Your Mind, and Your Heart

When you were a baby inside your mother's tummy, Creator gave you a perfect little heart, a perfect little mind, and a perfect little body. Your *Spirit* also came to you at that time. Some people call Spirit "*The Holy Spirit.*" All people, animals, plants, and everything Creator made, have a Spirit. In this chapter, I share more ways you can take good care of your Spirit, body, mind, and heart.

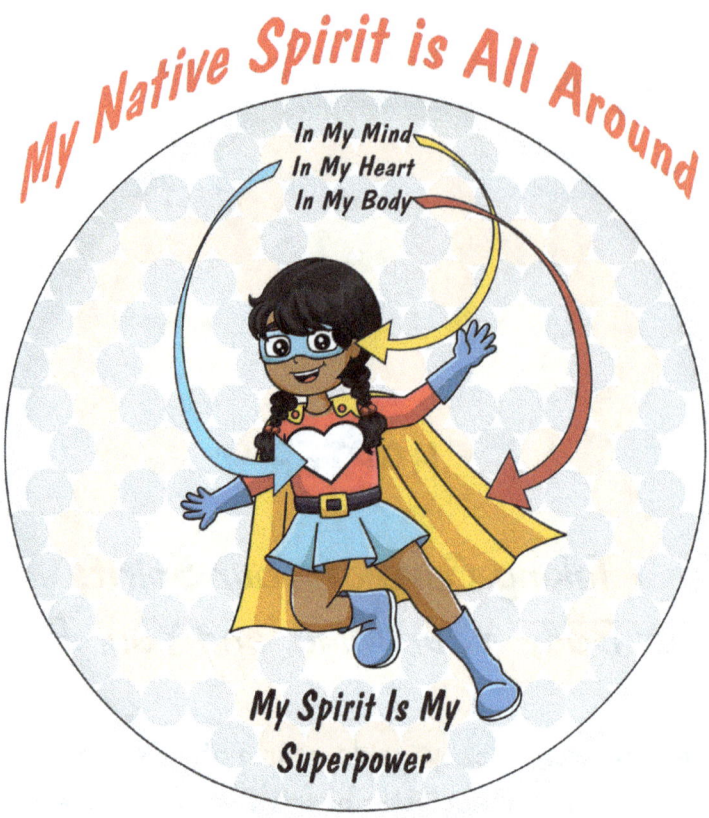

By: Geri Paul ©

Your Spirit is your superpower! Creator loves you so much he gifted you with your good body, a smart mind, a kind heart, and your Spirit. Creator surrounded you with warm and caring people, too.

It is very cool how your Spirit is connected to every part of you. Also, you are connected to Creator. Remember, you are allowed to take good care of your gifts. Let us begin by looking at taking care of your body.

Taking Care of Your Body

Creator made your body perfect. No one in the entire world has a body exactly like yours. Remember, when you take care of your body, you also take care of your mind, your heart, and your Spirit. You do this, all at the same time! Your body is your Spirit's home, so, it is important to take care of this special place.

Say To Yourself:

> I am a lovable kid, and I am allowed to take care of my body. Creator made my body just right, and I am allowed to love it!

Taking care of your body includes:
- Eating healthy *power food*
- Exercising every day
- Getting enough sleep
- Having good body hygiene
- Getting regular check-ups

Good Healthy Food

Power Food Gives Your Body Energy

The food you eat goes to every part of your body. Healthy food becomes energy and makes your entire body stronger, smarter, and faster. Unhealthy food weakens your body and stops you from performing your best.

Food breaks down and goes to your blood, muscles, organs, bones, and brain. When food is in your mouth and stomach it starts breaking down into energy. The power from the food goes into your blood and to every part of your body. The energy from your blood even goes to your brain!

On the next page is a list of healthy and unhealthy food. What are your favourite healthy foods? What do you enjoy eating the most that is unhealthy?

Good Food Makes You Strong
By: Geri Paul ©

It is okay to have a treat every now and again, but not too many and not too often.

UNHEALTHY FOOD

Fizzy Drinks
pop, sugary drinks

Fast Food
burgers, fries, greasy chicken

Junk Food
candy, potato chips, cookies

Processed Foods
boxed macaroni dinners,
hot dogs, canned processed meats

HEALTHY FOOD

Fruit / Nuts / Seeds
blueberries, bananas, almonds

Water

Meat
dry meat, fish, chicken, elk,
moose, caribou, seal

Vegetables
carrots, beans, spinach
salads, broccoli, tomato

Say to yourself: healthy food makes me strong.
Too much unhealthy food hurts my mind, my body,
my heart, and my Spirit.

Healthy Food Makes Your Entire Body Strong

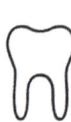   

Bones	Liver
Brain	Heart
Teeth	Lungs
Fingernails	Hair
Toenails	Eyes
Skin	Muscles
Kidneys	Veins
Stomach	Blood

Taking good care of your body also includes moving around and getting exercise every day. When you exercise, you take care of your body, mind, heart, and Spirit. This happens all at the same time. On the next page are a few physical activities you can try. Trying new things is great fun! If you think you will not like a new activity, try it anyway.

Fun Physical Activities

Running	Snow Shoeing
Walking	Working-out
Skateboarding	Hiking
Swimming	Basketball
Canoeing - Kayaking	Baseball
Riding Bike	Gymnastics
Dancing	Hockey
Playing at the Park	Football
Nature Walks	Pow-Wow Dancing
Treadmill Walks	Skiing
Wrestling	Hunting
Martial Arts-Karate	Horseback Riding

What are your favourite physical activities?

_____

What new activity would you like to try?

_____

Rest and Sleep

Getting enough rest and sleep are also crucial for your entire body, mind, and Spirit. Make sure you get at least nine to ten hours of sleep every night. Also, turn off all screens when you go to bed. Your body will love you for it! Without *enough* sleep and rest, the following can happen:

- You can become forgetful and think slowly.
- Your body can run out of energy, and you can start craving unhealthy food.
- You can also stop exercising.
- Almost everything can feel harder to do.
- Your body can get sick.
- You can also feel grumpy, angry, and sad.

Good Body Hygiene

Good body hygiene means keeping your entire body clean. This includes brushing your teeth daily, bathing-showering, combing your hair, and wearing clean clothes.

Getting Regular Check-ups

You should get regular check-ups, not just when you are hurting. Getting check-ups with the dentist, the doctor, and the optometrist (the eye doctor) are also important for your body. An adult needs to make these appointments for you. Also, tell an adult if your body hurts or you cannot see, hear, taste, or smell well.

Say To Yourself:

I have a lovable and good body. I am allowed to keep myself healthy and strong.

Here are four extra points to remember about your body.

1. You are allowed to love your body and take care of it daily.

2. Smile at yourself in the mirror and look for the good things. For example, notice your lovely eyes, shiny hair, and smile. Do not look for negative things.

3. If someone makes fun of how you look, tell yourself, "Creator made me, and my body is fine and good."

4. Tell an adult if someone is hurting you or saying mean things about your body.

> **Say To Yourself:**
> Taking care of my body is one way of being my own good friend.

Taking Care of Your Mind

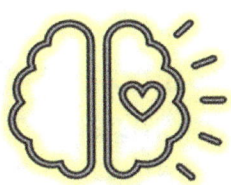

Next, we will talk about taking care of your mind. Taking care of your mind is just as important as taking care of your body. Your mind includes your thoughts, memories, and imagination. Your mind also includes your dreams and messages you give yourself.

Your mind is very powerful, amazing, and intelligent. On the following page is a chart outlining a few incredible things your mind can do. Read this chart and see if I forgot to mention any other things that make your mind amazing and smart.

Your Mind Is Amazing and Smart

- You can think and figure things out
- You can think and make good decisions
- You can stop bad thinking
- You can remember things

Your Mind Is Very Powerful

- You have a great imagination
- You can day dream
- You can dream in your sleep
- You can talk to yourself and be your own good friend
- You can visit places in your mind

By: Geri Paul ©

Twelve Ways to Take Care of Your Mind

Over the following few pages, I talk about ways you can take good care of your mind. I call these ways "*Mind-Power-Tools for Kids*." They include the following:

Mind-Power-Tools For Kids

1. Talk to yourself in good-positive ways
2. Keep reading and learning
3. Write
4. Get enough sleep and relaxation
5. Smudge and pray
6. Use your imagination
7. Eat healthy brain food
8. Do not use marijuana, alcohol, harmful drugs, bad pills, other substances, cigarettes or vapes
9. Talk to people who care about you
10. Take breaks from overthinking
11. Laugh a lot every day
12. Wear a helmet

I will now discuss each Mind-Power-Tool in a little more detail.

1. **Talk to yourself in good-positive ways**

    - Every now and again, stop and listen to your brain and notice how you talk to yourself. Stop any bad negative messages. Instead, practice talking to yourself in good-positive ways.

    - Tell yourself good messages and let yourself know you are a good kid. For example, when you make a mistake remind yourself that everyone makes mistakes. You are still a good person.

    - Practice saying **STOP** to yourself if you keep thinking bad negative thoughts. If you find yourself worrying a lot, tell yourself **STOP**. Replace bad thoughts with good ones. Tell yourself, "I will be OK. These are just thoughts", "My thoughts are not always true." Ask an adult to find extra help if you cannot stop your troubling thoughts.

2. **Keep learning and reading**

    - Read exciting books often.

    - Read and learn more about your Native identity, your Native culture, your Native language, and your family history.

    - Ask questions. Your questions are important. Do not worry whether other people already know the answers.

- Learn a new hobby like beading, cooking, hunting, a new sport, or a new game like chess.

- Try drawing or painting and make a self-portrait. A self-portrait is a picture of yourself.

3. **Write**

    - Write a story about something you love. For example, you can write about your pet or your favourite movie.

    - Write a song or a poem.

    - Write your thoughts in a journal.

    - Write yourself a friendly letter and talk to yourself like you would speak to a good friend.

4. **Get enough sleep and relaxation**

    - Get at least nine or more hours of sleep every night.

    - Practice a good bedtime routine. Turn off all screens 30 minutes before bedtime, brush your teeth, clean your skin, pray, and relax.

    - Do not watch too much TV or play too many video games.

    - Do not stay on your phone too long.

5. Smudge and pray

- Smudge and pray every morning, and as often as you need. Ask Creator to keep your mind strong and healthy.

- Go to Native ceremonies or church.

- Ask someone to teach you Native singing and drumming.

6. Eat healthy brain food

- Drink water instead of pop.

- Eat fruit and vegetables.

- Cut back on sugary food and junk food.

- Eat less fast food and processed meat.

7. Use your imagination

- Relax in a peaceful place, like in nature or your bedroom, and visit your good memories.

- Daydream about doing one of your favourite things like skateboarding, spending time with people you are fond of, and snuggling with your dog or cat.

- Practice deep breathing (breathe in good thoughts and breathe out bad ones). Breathe in slowly, all the way to your belly button and hold your breath for three seconds. Let your breath out slowly through your nose. Do this five times.

8. **Do not use marijuana, alcohol, harmful drugs, wrong pills, other substances, or cigarettes**

9. **Talk to people who care about you**

    - Visit and talk to kids and adults who love and care about you.

    - Talk to an adult you trust if you have bad or scary thoughts or dreams.

    - Spend time with animals.

10. **Take breaks from overthinking**

    - When you think too much, take a break. You can walk, ride a bike, visit a good friend, or spend time with family. Focus on your activity and say to yourself, "My *over-thinking* is on hold for a while. I am going to enjoy myself right now and focus on what I am doing."

11. **Laugh a lot every day**

    - Watch a funny movie or make a funny video with friends.

    - Have fun with your family and friends. For example, you can play fun board games, share funny memories (start by saying, "remember the time when …").

    - Read funny stories and tell funny jokes.

12. **Wear a helmet**

- Your brain can bruise and bleed if you bump it hard enough. Always wear a helmet when doing activities where you can fall, slip, or get bumped.

- Here are a few examples of when you should wear a helmet: when riding a bike, a scooter, a quad, a dirt bike, a snowmobile, skiing, playing certain sports, ice skating, skateboarding, horseback riding, and rodeoing. What other times should you wear a helmet?

Your Body is a Home for Your Spirit

Your Heart is a Heater and Keeps You Warm, It Holds Your Feelings

Your Mind Holds Your Thoughts

Taking Care of Your Heart

You were born with a warm and kind heart

We already discussed ways to take good care of your body and mind. Over the following few pages, I will share ways you can take good care of your heart. The best person to do this is you!

Remember, Creator made your heart special in many ways. For example, when you were a baby, Creator filled your heart with love and kindness. Creator also made your heart like a *heater* which keeps your body toasty warm. Your heart is also *magical*. Sharing your love and kindness with others magically helps them feel toasty warm, too. As well, the more you share, the bigger and warmer your heart grows.

Make sure you take good care of your heart. On the following two pages is a list of suggestions to help you. I call this list *22 Power-Tools For A Kid's Heart*. Some tips will sound familiar, as I have already mentioned them in earlier chapters.

Say To Yourself:

I am allowed to share my love and kindness. I am also allowed to take care of my heart and ask for help when my heart hurts.

22 Power-Tools For A Kid's Heart

1. Ask for Help When You Feel a Heartache or Upset
2. Talk to Creator
3. Smile at Yourself in the Mirror
4. Become Your Own Good Friend
5. Forgive Yourself When You Make Mistakes, and Apologize When You Hurt Someone
6. You Do Not Need To Be Perfect
7. Smile When You See Someone You Know
8. Carry an Imaginary Person on Your Shoulder
9. Celebrate Someone Else's Happiness
10. Spend Time in Nature
11. Be a Kid. Let Yourself Take Breaks, Laugh, Play, and Do Kid Things
12. Kiss and Hug Someone You Know Well and Love. Tell Them Kind Words
13. Make a Card or Picture for Someone
14. Practice Being Kind to Your Family
15. Spend Time With Animals
16. Learn to Play a New Instrument Like Guitar, Piano, Flute, Violin, or Drums
17. Practice or Learn Pow-Wow Singing and Dancing

18. Do Traditional Things - Go to Native Ceremonies and Events
19. Share
20. Do Not Let Anyone Take Advantage of Your Heart and Kindness
21. Tell an Adult if You are Sick, Hungry, or if Someone is Hurting Your Body or Heart
22. Use Your Imagination; Go Somewhere You Always Dreamed of Going.

I will now discuss each power-tool in a little more detail.

1. **Ask for help when you feel a heartache or upset**

    - Here are three examples of how to ask for help when your heart is hurting and when you feel upset. You can say:

    - "I feel upset right now. I need a hug."

    - "I feel sad and lonely, and do not want to be alone. Can you stay with me?"

    - "My heart hurts. Can we talk?"

2. **Talk to Creator**

    - Tell Creator what is inside your heart. He is always listening; he wants to hear how you are feeling and help you.

3. **Smile at yourself in the mirror**

    - Look for the good things about yourself.

    - Do not look for bad things, and do not tell yourself bad-negative messages.

4. **Become your own good friend**

    - Treat yourself with love and kindness. Do not beat yourself up when you make mistakes.

5. **Forgive yourself when you make mistakes, and apologize when you hurt someone**

    - Tell yourself, "Even though I made a mistake, I forgive myself. I am still a good and lovable kid."

    - Tell the person you hurt or made a mistake to that you are sorry.

    - Tell yourself, "Making mistakes helps me learn and grow stronger."

6. **You do not need to be perfect**

    - Trying your best is much more important than trying to be flawless.

    - Say to yourself, "I do not need to be perfect. I need to try my best."

7. Smile when you see someone you know

    - When you see a person you know, greet them with a smile.

    - When you meet someone new, greet them with a smile, too. Do not ignore someone when they speak to you, turn your head, or walk away.

8. Carry an imaginary person on your shoulder

    - Carry a pretend friend, mother, father, grandmother, or grandfather on your shoulder. Have your pretend person give you kind messages such as: "You are doing a good job", "Keep trying hard, and you will make it", and "You are smart and awesome, and I am proud of you."

9. Celebrate someone else's happiness

    - When someone does well, like winning an award or getting nice things, celebrate their happiness. For example, you can tell the person you are happy for them, or you are proud of them.

    - Do not ignore any angry or jealous feelings you experience. Remind yourself that feeling angry or jealous does not mean you are a bad kid. It usually means you need to talk to an adult about your feelings.

10. Spend time in nature

    - Spending time in nature is important.

    - When you cannot go outside, you can look through your window and notice the trees, the birds, and the clouds. You can also read many wonderful and exciting books about nature.

    - Notice the little things like the colour of birds and the different types of trees. Some birds are blue, and others are black, red, grey, or white. Some trees are tall, and others are chubby. Notice the shapes in the clouds. Study little ants around your home and notice how they walk. Figure out what they are doing.

11. Be a kid. Let yourself take breaks, laugh, play, and do kid things

    Blow bubbles, swing, skip rope, or play with your dog. Skateboard, run, ride a bike, or go sledding in the snow.

12. Kiss and hug someone you know well and love. Tell them kind words

    - You can hug or kiss a baby, a brother or sister, a cousin, an aunt or uncle, a friend, a parent, or a grandparent.

13. Make a card or picture for someone

14. Practice being kind to your family

    - Offer to help where you can. Do not wait to be asked; offer to help make the bed and tidy the living room or your bedroom.

    - Apologize to your relative when you make a mistake.

    - Give someone in your family a hug or say kind words when they feel sad or if they are having a bad day. You can make a card or a drawing telling them you love them and care.

    - Visit healthy family and friends.

        - You can visit, call, or facetime a friend, a cousin, an aunt or uncle, or a parent or grandparent.

15. Spend time with animals

    - Hug and snuggle your dog or cat. Talk to your bird, hamster, or fish. Take your dog for a walk.

16. Learn to play a new instrument like guitar, piano, flute, violin, or drums

    - If you cannot attend classes, there are many free online lessons.

- Ask an adult to help you explore ways to learn a new instrument.

- Perhaps a family friend or relative can teach you.

17. Practice or learn pow-wow singing and dancing

- Ask family or friends whether they dance or sing and if they can teach you.

- There are also many online lessons to help you get started.

- You can practice in your own home and do not need to have an entire outfit to begin dancing or singing.

18. Go to Native ceremonies and events

- I talk much more about this in Chapter 10.

19. Share

- When you share, you help people feel good, and your heart grows bigger and warmer, too.

- You can share many things like your kind words, toys, snacks, and favourite stories.

20. Do not let anyone take advantage of your heart and kindness

    - Sometimes you need to say "no" to friends and other people. For example, do not let other kids take your money or things, bully you, or boss you around.

    - Should someone keep asking for your money, food, clothes, or toys, you are allowed to say, "No, I do not want to do that."; or, you can say "Please stop asking me, I cannot keep doing that."

21. Tell an adult if you are sick, hungry, or if someone is hurting you or your heart

    - If the adult does not help, ask another adult. Never stop asking for help.

22. Use your imagination; go somewhere you always dreamed of going

    - You can go anywhere in your mind. You can go to the mountains, lie on a beach, swim in the ocean, or hang out with your favourite people.

    - You can also pretend you are riding a bike or a horse, fishing, or visiting another country.

Say To Yourself:

- I am lovable, and I am allowed to take good care of my heart.
- I am allowed to let myself play and laugh and be a kid.
- I am allowed to make mistakes.
- I am allowed to share my love and kindness.
- I am allowed to say "no" to people who try and take advantage of my heart.

You did an excellent job reading this section! I am proud of you!

Indigenous Self-Care Wheel

You do not need to re-read this entire chapter to get the self-care information we already discussed. Instead, I include an Indigenous *Self-Care Wheel* to help you.

You can see a lot in this one-page snapshot. This wheel includes ideas to help you take care of your body, mind, and heart. There is a section for the people in your world, too. Ideas for taking care of your Spirit are also inside and around the circle.

Ask someone to photocopy this wheel and tape it on a wall or the refrigerator. I will talk more about using this self-care tool on page 250 and 251.

Indigenous Self-Care Wheel

Pray & Smudge Every Day

Spirit — *Spirit*

HEART
- Play & be a kid
- Feel all your feelings the good & not-so-good
- Share your love & be kind
- Thank Creator every day
- Be a friend to yourself
- Talk good to yourself
- Listen to music
- Smile a lot
- Spend time with animals
- Hug someone you love
- Walk in nature

BODY
- Drink more water
- Eat healthy
- Do not eat too many treats
- Exercise every day
- Sleep 9+ hours each night
- Keep your body, teeth, & clothes clean
- Do not use cigarettes, marijuana, alcohol, bad pills, or drugs
- Get check-ups with the doctor, dentist, & eye doctor

CREATOR

MIND
- Read exciting books
- Try new things
- Learn your Native culture & language
- Practice deep breathing
- Say "STOP" to control scary thoughts
- Tell yourself nice messages like, "I am a lovable kid"
- Limit your screentime
- Limit your videogames

PEOPLE
- See people who make you feel good
- Never keep bad secrets
- Be kind to others & yourself
- Do not let people take your money & things
- Tell an adult you trust if you are hurt, scared, bullied, or sick

Spirit — *Spirit*

Go To Ceremony
Be Proud of Your Native Culture

By: Geri Paul ©

Use the Indigenous Self-Care Wheel in the following ways:

1. You can use this wheel when you feel upset or have any not-so-good feelings.

   For example, if someone is bullying you, look under the *People* section of the wheel and see what you can do to make yourself feel better.

   Under the *People* section, you will read, "Never keep bad secrets", and "Tell an adult you trust if you are hurt, scared, bullied, or sick."

2. You can use this wheel to remind yourself that Creator is the centre of *your* life, just like he is shown in the centre of this wheel. Creator touches every part of you, and he never leaves you.

3. This wheel can also be a reminder to smudge, pray, and attend Native ceremonies or church.

4. Remember, when you see the word "Spirit" on the wheel, this is a reminder that your Spirit is all around you. You are never alone; your Spirit also lives in every part of you. This is a great thing!

5. When you look at the self-care wheel, you can also remind yourself that every part of you is connected.

Taking care of one area will affect others. For example, when you take care of your body, you automatically take care of your mind, heart, and Spirit. The people in your world will also feel happy when you take care of yourself.

6. Finally, you are welcome to share this wheel with your family and friends. This self-care tool is meant for everyone, including adults.

I will now move on to the final chapter of this book. In Chapter 10, I summarize many things we have already discussed. I also talk more about being proud of your Native identity and colonization.

CHAPTER 10

Conclusion and Being Proud of Your Native Identity

The more you learn about your Native culture, the more you will know yourself. Being proud of who you are and where you came from are your superpowers! In this last chapter, I summarize much of what we have discussed already. I will also explain more ways you can stay in touch with your Native culture. As well, I include extra information on colonization and how you can use your superpowers to fight racism.

Learn More About Your Native Culture: Family and Ancestors

You are a lovable kid, and you deserve to know your Native culture and family. As I mentioned in Chapter 1, your Native tribe and family are not the same as every other Native tribe and family. It is, therefore, important to keep learning about your community and family traditions. At the same time, remember, it is exciting to keep learning about other Native cultures, too. The more you know about your own culture and others, the more you also learn about yourself.

> **Say To Yourself:**
> I am important to this world and deserve to know my Native culture. I am allowed to be my own good friend and feel proud of my Native identity.

Native tribes all over the world have many things that are the same. For example, most Native cultures believe in Creator and the Spirits. They also share a great respect for their language, the land, the animals, and all of life.

Native tribes all over the world also have many things that are different. Native people living in the same province, or the same state, sometimes speak different Native languages and have different ways of living. For example, different tribes have unique ways of doing ceremonies and events. They also have their own ways of dressing, hunting, and preparing food.

Your Native tribe is special because they, too, have unique ways of living. Keep learning as much as you can about your tribe. For example, you can start learning more about your culture by asking family and friends what they know about the following topics.

- Ceremony
- Protocols
- Traditional Medicines
- Traditional Food
- Hunting and Fishing
- Singing & Dancing
- Carving & Artwork
- Traditional Clothing
- Types of Homes
- Ways of Travel
- Traditional Land
- Native Language
- Colonization

Learn About Ceremony, Protocol, and Traditional Medicines

Ceremony - There are many ceremonies you can learn about and possibly attend. Ask whether your community has naming ceremonies, sweat lodges, night lodges, bundle openings, sundances, societal ceremonies, pipe ceremonies, and drumming and singing ceremonies. There are many other ceremonies you can also find out about.

As well, ask about your tribe's creation stories. Learn how Creator gave your people medicines, language, and the sweat lodge. You can find out more about sacred locations and items like feathers, bundles, pipes, drums, and rattles. There are also so many more important and exciting things you can learn about.

Protocol — You need to learn about proper protocols when attending **Native** events and ceremonies. Protocols are like the rules and practices people follow.

Following correct protocol is extremely important because it shows our respect to Creator and the Spirits. We also honour Creator when we use proper protocols and ask for help in *good ways*.

Remember, there are many protocols and knowing them can take a lifetime. No one is perfect, and we are allowed to make mistakes when learning.

Also, every tribe has their own protocols which probably differ from other tribes. Here are a few examples of when you can ask an Elder or an adult about using protocols.

- When gathering or using traditional medicines

- When hunting

- When making some traditional clothing, headdresses, drums, rattles, and other items

- When preparing certain ceremonial food

- When seeking Elder's help

- When seeking ceremonial and traditional knowledge

- When attending ceremonies such as funerals, weddings, sweat lodges, night lodges, pipe ceremonies, naming ceremonies, sundances, and many others

Traditional Medicines - Native people have been using traditional medicines since the beginning of time. Medicines are great gifts from Creator. Every tribe has medicines growing right on their land. Some medicines only grow in certain places; therefore, Native people still trade and share their medicines, just as they did long ago. Sharing like this is a beautiful thing! Medicines include sage, sweetgrass, cedar, tobacco, juniper, sweet pine, fungus, different tree bark, and many other plants and roots.

There are hundreds of medicines used for many purposes. Some medicines are for pain and sicknesses. Others are for smudging, cleansing, and for using in many Native ceremonies. People usually need teachings, and sometimes special rights, to gather and use certain medicines. You can learn your tribe's medicines and see whether you can help gather some. Remember to ask an Elder or a family member about the protocol you need to follow before you begin picking.

Learn About Food, Hunting, and Fishing

Traditional Food - There is a lot to learn about traditional food and how to gather and prepare them. For example, you can learn how to dry and smoke meat and fish. You can also learn to gather and prepare berries, wild rice, and other traditional plants, herbs, and roots. Remember, gathering and preparing some ceremonial food require proper protocol.

Hunting and Fishing - Learning how your people hunted and fished in the past is very exciting. For example, you can find out how people hunted buffalo, elk, deer, moose, rabbits, beaver, and birds. You can also learn how hunting seal and dolphin is different than hunting land animals like elk or moose. Compare how your people hunt and fish today to how they hunted and fished a long time ago.

Learn About Singing, Dancing, and Artwork

Singing, Dancing, and Artwork - Something else important and exciting to learn is your tribe's traditional songs and dances. For example, learn how to pow-wow dance and sing the beautiful pow-wow songs. There are also many new ways of singing, dressing, and dancing at pow-wows today. Native people have always loved dancing and singing. It is such great fun!

You can also learn about beautiful Native artwork like beading and drawing. Gathering more information on carvings made from soapstone, antlers, and bones is also very exciting and important. Ask about totem poles, drum and rattle making, and basket weaving. There are many important stories that go with learning traditional artwork. See whether you can learn these teachings and stories.

Learn About Clothing, Homes, and Travel

Clothing - It is wonderful learning how Native people all over the world dress. Every tribe has their own beautiful clothing styles. Find out how your ancestors dressed. Did your people wear clothes made of seal skin, deer, elk, or buffalo hides? What kind of clothing did they wear during the summer and winter? Did the children wear special clothes, or did they dress the same as the adults? You can even learn to tan animal skins and make traditional clothing if you like.

Types of Homes - Learning about the types of homes your family and ancestors lived in is also exciting. For example, find out whether they lived in tipis, igloos, or wigwams. Did they change homes during the summer and winter?

Ways of Travel - Discovering how your people travelled is also very cool. Did they travel using husky dog teams with komatiks? Did they use horses and boats, or did they travel mostly by walking?

You can learn much more besides what I cover in this chapter. For instance, you can get to know more about your tribe's language and study traditional land territories and your Native treaty rights. Ask an adult to help you understand these topics.

You are Always Learning

Understanding more about your Native culture is never boring because you will never know everything. There is always something new to learn. Also, you do not need to try and understand too much at once. Remember, your learning is a life-long journey that never ends. Keep listening and asking questions. All your thoughts are important; there are no wrong questions.

If you like, you can write down three things you are most interested in learning about *right now*.

1. _____   2. _____   3. _____

Also, you can write down three things you are interested in learning about *later*.

1. _____   2. _____   3. _____

Say To Yourself:

Learning more about my culture and other Native cultures is important. Learning teaches me more about myself, my family, and other Native people.

On the following two pages, is a list of questions you can use when discovering more about your Native tribe. You can also use these questions when learning about other tribes, too. This list is like the one I mentioned in Chapter 1.

Questions You Can Ask When Learning More About Your Native Tribe

➤ Where did your Native ancestors live?

➤ Where do your people live today?

➤ What Native language did they speak?

➤ What ceremonies and protocols did your family practice in the past?

➤ What ceremonies and protocols do they practice today?

➤ What traditional food did your people eat in the past?

➤ What traditional food do they eat today?

➤ What are the traditional medicines your tribe used in the past?

➤ What traditional medicines do they use today?

➤ What songs did they sing in the past?

➤ What songs do they sing today?

➤ What kind of dancing did they do in the past?

➤ What kind of dancing do they do today?

> What kinds of artwork and crafts did they make in the past?

> What artwork and crafts do they make today?

> What kind of traditional clothing did they wear in the past?

> What traditional clothing do they wear today?

> How has colonization affected your family and community in the past?

> How does colonization affect your family and community today?

In the next section, I talk more about colonization and how it causes a lot of hurt for Native people.

Colonization Causes A Lot of Problems and Hurt for Native People Everywhere

Learning about *colonization* means understanding how Native people are affected by people who invade Native land. What you are about to read is sad and tragic. However, you must know how Native people suffer from colonization, racism, and abuse. Knowing the truth will help you understand more about yourself and your family. Knowing the truth will also help you understand the struggles many Native people all over the world face.

There are many books and information written about colonization. Make sure you keep learning about this subject as I cover just a few points in this book.

A Few Things to Know About Colonization

- Colonization happens when non-Native people invade the land where Native people live.

- Native people all over the world suffer from colonization.

- Colonization happened in the past and keeps happening today.

- Colonizer's goals included taking as much Native territory as possible. They wanted the land, animals, forests, and oceans.

- Great amounts of land were taken and many Native communities in Canada and the United States were destroyed.

- Another goal colonizers had was to stop Native people from being themselves. They wanted Native people to turn as White as possible; they believed their ways of living were better than Native ways.

- Therefore, colonizers tried to destroy everything that was Native. They wanted all Native traditions, languages, ceremonies, and ways of living destroyed.

- Colonizers tried very hard to break Native people's Spirits.

- Some colonizers wanted to "kill off" the Native race completely. Killing off a race of people on purpose is called *genocide*.

- For example, it is shocking to know that colonizers tried to stop Native people from having more babies.

- Doctors and nurses did this by sterilizing Native women and teenage girls without their permission. This means a procedure was performed so women could not have children.

- Native women were tricked into believing other procedures were happening instead of sterilization.

- When Native people tried to stop the colonizers, thousands of them were killed.

- Another example of genocide includes the deliberate killing of Native people. Some tribes were killed off entirely while protecting their family and culture.

- For example, genocide happened when every Elder, adult, teenager, child, and baby were killed in the Beothuk tribe. The Beothuk Indians lived in central Newfoundland, Canada. Sadly, there are no more Beothuk people today.

- Also, the colonizers used their education, religion, and abuse to further control and trick Native people.

- For example, the government's people tricked and lied to Native people when the land treaties were created. They stole much land because Native leaders could not read the documents that were written in English. The English documents included different things than what Native leaders agreed to during talks.

- The colonizer's plans further included taking away Native people's freedom. Entire communities were forced to live on land called reservations. Native people needed special permission from government agents to leave the reservations. They were prisoners on their own land.

- Without land and freedom, Native people could no longer work or travel as they did in the past. Such horrible circumstances stopped Native people from providing safe homes, healthy food, and warm clothing for their children and families.

- As well, Native people were punished and arrested for speaking their Native languages and practicing sacred ceremonies.

- Many thousands of Native people also died from starvation and diseases the colonizers carried.

- The above conditions, plus much more, caused many Native men and women to lose their confidence as proud Native warriors and providers.

Taking Children From Their Families

Colonizers also took Native children from their homes and families. When parents fought to keep their children, the police punished them or sent them to prison.

Residential and Day Schools

- Residential and day schools were all over Canada and the United States. These schools were sometimes called *Indian Boarding Schools*.

- Tens of thousands of Native children were abducted and forced to attend residential and day schools.

- Your relatives may have gone as they were in operation for a long time.

- This was a devastating time for the children, their families, and entire Native communities.

- It is also shocking and sad to learn how the little children suffered in these schools.

Abuse at Residential and Day Schools

- Adults working at the schools abused the children in every way.

- The abusers included teachers, priests, fathers, nuns, and holy sisters and brothers. Other adults who worked in the schools, churches, hospitals, and the government also abused the children.

- Children were heartbroken, scared, beaten, and punished in very cruel ways.

- A lot of children went hungry and became very sick. Many children died because the treatment was so horrible.

- For example, the children were brutally beaten, punished, and starved if they did not pray and act like the colonizers.

- The colonizers wanted to destroy all traces of the children's Native identity.

- So, they cut their beautiful hair short and stopped them from wearing their beautiful Native clothes. The children were forced to wear colonizer's clothing instead.

- Children were forced to work very hard and had to do work meant for adults.

- Many little children were also sexually abused by the holy men and women at the schools and churches.

- The sexual abusers included the church's fathers, priests, nuns, brothers, and sisters.

- Other teachers and workers at the schools, hospitals, and government sexually abused the children as well.

- Colonizers believed Native children were dirty savages and heathens. They poked fun at the children's physical appearance, called them terrible names, and put down their Native culture and families.

- The children were held hostage and were not allowed to leave the schools.

- As well, children were no longer allowed to use their traditional Native names.

- Traditional names were important because this is how children identified themselves.

- The children's traditional names were also their connection to Creator and their Spirit. The colonizers did not want Native children to have their traditional connection to Creator, so they renamed every child with White names.

- It was also against the rules for children to speak their Native languages and pray to Creator.

- Stopping children from speaking their language also prevented them from connecting with their people and with their "*Source of Life and Native Spirit.*"

- As well, children were often separated from their brothers and sisters and not allowed to speak to them.

- Some children did escape and returned to their families. However, most were caught and forced back to the residential and day schools. They were severely punished upon their return.

- Sadly, as well, not all children who escaped made it home. Many children died along the way.

- There are no more residential or day schools like those from the past. However, Native people are still hurting because the trauma keeps living inside of them.

Discovering Children's Secret Graves

- It is terrible how people at the residential schools buried little children and wanted to keep their deaths secret.

- Today, thousands of little children's remains are found in massive graves. Many more are still being discovered.

- These graves are near old residential school land. This is very sad.

- Colonizers planted trees over some graves and hoped their horrible sins would never be discovered.

- However, parents and families always knew something horrible had happened to their missing children. Their hearts and Spirits told them.

- When parents fought or questioned the colonizers about their missing children, they were often severely punished or arrested.

Colonizers Could Not Take Everything

Fortunately, the colonizers could not take everything away. Native people always kept their powerful Spirits and they refused to give up on their children and culture. As a result, some Native languages, traditions, and ceremonies are here today.

- For example, some families hid their children and continued teaching them **Native** ways.

- They kept speaking their Native languages, and they kept practicing their ceremonies in secret.

- This meant Native people held their ceremonies at night or in private places, away from the police. If people were caught, they would have been severely punished, sent to prison, or in some cases, killed.

Many Native people today are grateful to their relatives because they **Never Gave Up on Creator and their Native Identity.**

Colonization Today

Some non-Native people bully and lie to Native people. They take Native land, and they take their children.

Racism hurts Native people and stops many from getting a good education, and finding work to pay their bills.

World problems happened before you or your parents were born. These big problems keep damaging Native people and their families today.

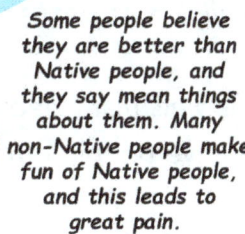

Racism makes some Native people feel bad about themselves, and they feel ashamed of their Native culture.

Some people believe they are better than Native people, and they say mean things about them. Many non-Native people make fun of Native people, and this leads to great pain.

By: Geri Paul ©

Colonization today does not look the same as it did in the past. There are no more residential schools like those in the past, for example, and Native people are no longer held hostage on their reservations.

- However, colonization keeps happening. Native people all over the world are still hurting and are treated poorly by many non-Native people.

- Too many people continue believing they are better than Native people. They believe they are greater in every way, including physically, mentally, emotionally, Spiritually, culturally, and socially.

- For example, a great number of people still believe their religion is better than Native Spirituality. *Remember though, Creator loves everybody, and he does not pick any religion as better than another.*

- As well, many people today keep bullying and trying to trick Native people out of land and other valuable resources.

- Colonization also happens when people try to trick Native people into giving them cultural and ceremonial information. People sometimes want Native knowledge for the wrong reasons. For example, they want Native information to make money or to make themselves look powerful.

More Ways Colonization Continues Causing Damage

Below are a few more examples of how colonization and racism keep happening.

- Racism stops many people from feeling confident and proud of their Native identity. Too many people are ashamed of their Native heritage, and they sometimes try to hide being Native.

- When Native people are discriminated against, many will also try and ease their hurt by using alcohol and drugs. Abusing substances leads to more hurt, violence, and other forms of abuse.

- Also, many companies are still racist and will not hire Native people.

- As well, racism prevents many people from getting a good education. For instance, in non-Native schools, students and school staff still pick on and bully Native children.

- New *modern forms of school racism* include leaving Native kids out of activities on purpose. Teachers and others also embarrass Native kids in front of the class.

- As well, teachers sometimes grade Native kids unfairly.

- Non-Native students continue attacking Native kids. Teachers and staff turn a blind eye and pretend nothing happened.

- Staff and students also call Native kids terrible names. They make humiliating insults about their family and culture.

There are many more forms of modern racism besides what I mention in this book. Today's *modern* colonization and racism is extremely damaging and play a big role in Native people's suffering.

Fighting Colonization and Racism Use Your Superpowers!

Now that you understand a little more about colonization, please **do not fill your heart with hatred or revenge toward colonizers and non-Native people.**

It is true that colonization and racism hurt Native communities, families, and kids. It can leave children and teenagers feeling insecure, mad, hopeless, sad, and not as important as other kids. Remember, when you think about colonization and racism, you are allowed to experience all your feelings.

Also remember, the best way to fight colonization and racism includes using your superpowers. Your superpowers include the following:

1. Stay close to Creator/God.

2. Focus on your healing and love yourself.

3. Love your Native identity and keep learning about your culture.

4. Stand up to bullies and abusers in smart and healthy ways.

5. Focus on your education; keep learning.

Please remember, filling your mind and heart with hatred and revenge will stop your superpowers. When you feel angry and hurt, talk to someone. All your feelings are important.

Sharing in a safe and caring place is healing. For example, you can talk to the adult reading with you. Discuss the feelings that come up when you think about colonization and racism. You can use the Indigenous Feelings Chart on the following page to help you. Talk about your feelings for as long as you need.

Indigenous Feelings Chart
How are you feeling?

Good Feelings

Not-So-Good Feelings

By: Geri Paul ©

Say To Yourself:

- I will ask for help when I am hurt.
- Healing and loving myself is the best!
- I am a lovable kid.
- I will be proud of my Native culture.
- I will not talk badly to myself.
- I will treat myself with kindness.
- No one is allowed to abuse or bully me.
- I will learn to fight colonization and racism with my superpowers!

When Native people keep healing and treating each other with kindness, a big change can happen. You play a very important part in this change. You are our future, and the world needs you!

More Healing, Right Now

You can add to your healing right now by noticing good things about yourself. What good things do you like about yourself?

- ✓ Your powerful Spirit
- ✓ Your gifts from Creator
- ✓ Your Native culture and community
- ✓ Your family, your ancestors
- ✓ Your smart brain
- ✓ Your kind and caring heart
- ✓ Your personality
- ✓ Your imagination
- ✓ Your face, your smile
- ✓ The colour of your skin, hair, and eyes
- ✓ Your body
- ✓ Your feelings

Name some other things you like about yourself _____.

Say To Yourself: My beauty comes from my inside. Being kind to myself and other people makes me beautiful.

A Note to You From the Author

Before I finish this chapter, I want to let you know that I am proud of you for doing your self-care and healing work. You are doing an excellent job! If you like, you can reread the helpful parts of this book. Also, if you ever feel scared or alone, remember, there are people who care about you. They want to help you. Keep reaching out. You can also talk and pray to Creator at any time. If you are unsure of how to pray, I include a prayer on the last page of this chapter. Use this prayer whenever you like, and never stop your good self-care.

Also, remember, when you make mistakes, it does not mean you are a bad kid. Even when you make big or small mistakes, Creator and other people love you. You are a lovable kid.

Even if we never meet, please know, I am sending you my love and good wishes inside this little heart!

With Love, Geri

Say To Yourself:

I am important to my family and community. I will use my superpowers to fight racism and abuse. My superpowers include **my healing, Creator, education, my Native identity, and standing up to abusers in smart and healthy ways.**

Some Things to Remember About Your Prayer

➢ You are allowed to ask for Creator's help.

➢ You can pray anytime and anywhere.

➢ You can make your prayer as long or as short as you want.

➢ Every prayer is correct. There is no wrong way to pray. Use your own words.

➢ Pray from your heart. Praying from your heart means saying how you feel.

➢ It is normal to wonder whether Creator is listening to you. Creator always listens, and he loves hearing from you.

➢ Sometimes it takes time to have your prayers answered. Be patient.

➢ Some people begin praying by saying their name. Your Native/Spiritual/Indian name is your connection to Creator and the Spirits. Ask an Elder about getting a Native name if you do not have one.

Children's Prayer

Dear Creator

My name is _____.

Thank you for my life and for giving me my body, my mind, my heart, and my Spirit. Thank you for loving me, and for making me important to this world.

I pray for the earth, the plants, and all the animals. I pray for all the holy things, the ceremonies, and the medicines you gave to help us. I pray you keep our Elders strong so they can keep teaching us about your good ways.

Creator, I would like you to help my family and friends (ask Creator for the kind of help you would like for them).

Creator, I would also like you to help me (fill in your own words here and ask Creator for what you need. Pray in your own way. Creator will understand. He likes it when you talk to him).

Thank you, Creator, for hearing my prayer today. I love you, and I will talk to you very soon.

By: Geri Paul ©

Call 911 if you or someone you know tries to take their own life.

Call 911 if you or someone you know is overdosing.

Call The Kids Helpline or text them any time. They are open 24-7 and they want to help you. Look online for the number or call zero (0) and ask.

REFERENCES

Chapter 1 — Native People, Culture and Birth Family

Conrad, M., Finkel, A. (2002). *History of the Canadian Peoples* (3rd. ed.). Pearson Education Canada Inc.

Cross, T. L. (2001). Spirituality and mental health: A Native American perspective. *Focal Point Fall, 15*(2), 37-38. https://www.pathwaysrtc.pdx.edu/pdf/fpF0124.pdf

Day, P. (2016). Raising healthy American Indian children: An Indigenous perspective. In H.N. Weaver (ed.). *Social Issues in Contemporary Native America: Reflections from Turtle Island* (pp. 93-112). Ashgate.

Falcon, C. L. Native cultural consultation for designing the Canada and US maps (personal communication, Jan 23, 2022; June 14, 2022; Jan 15, 2023).

Flanagan, T. (2005). *First Nations? Second Thoughts.* McGill-Queen's University Press.

Friesen, J. W. (1999). *First Nations of the Plains.* Detsilig Enterprises Ltd.

Friesen, J.W. (1997). *Rediscovering the First Nations of Canada.* Detsilig Enterprises Ltd.

Government of Canada. (2022, February). *Indigenous peoples and land (Map room).* https://www.rcaanc-cirnac.gc.ca/eng/ 1605796363328/1605796417543

Indian Lands of Federally Recognized Tribes of the United States. (2021, June). https://www.bia.gov/sites/default/files/dup/assets/bia/ots/webteam/pdf/idc1-028635.pdf

Kickett-Tucker, C., Christensen, D., Lawrence, D., Zubrick, S. R., Johnson, D. J., & Stanley, R. (2015). Development and validation of the Australian Aboriginal racial identity and self-esteem survey for 8-12-year-old children (IRISE_C). *International Journal for Equity in Health 14*(103). https://doi.org/10.1186/s12939-015-0234-3

Verhoeven, M., Poorthuis, A.M.G. & Volman, M. (2019). The role of school in adolescents' identity development: A literature review. *Educational Psychology Review 31*, 35–63. https://doi.org/10.1007/s10648-018-9457-3

Chapter 2 – Living Away from Your Birth Family

Allison-Burbank, J.D., & Collins, A. (2020). American Indian and Alaska Native fathers and their sacred children. In: Fitzgerald, H.E., von Klitzing, K., Cabrera, N.J., Scarano de Mendonça, J., & Skjøthaug, T. (eds). *Handbook of Fathers and Child Development*, 521-536. https://doi.org/10.1007/978-3-030-51027-5_31

Anderson, M. (2014). Protecting the rights of Indigenous and multicultural children and preserving their cultures in fostering and adoption. *The Journal of the Association of Family and Conciliation Courts 52*(1), 6-27. https://doi.org/10.1111/fcre.12067

Dalton L, Rapa E, Ziebland S, Rochat T, Kelly B, Hanington, L., Bland, R., Yousafzai, A., & Stein, A. (2019). Communication with children and adolescents about the diagnosis of a life-threatening condition in their parent. *Lancet, 393*(10176), 1164–1176. https://pubmed.ncbi.nlm.nih.gov/30894272

Ewing D. L., Monsen J. J., Thompson E. J., Cartwright-Hatton S., & Field A. (2013). A meta-analysis of transdiagnostic cognitive therapy in the treatment of child and young person anxiety disorders. *Behavioral and Cognitive Psychotherapy. 43*, 562–577. http://doi.org/10.1017/S1352465813001094

McQuaid, R.J, Schwartz, F.D., Blackstock, C., Matheson, K., Anisman, H., & Bombay, A. (2022). Parent-child separations and mental health among First Nations and Métis peoples in Canada: Links to intergenerational residential school attendance. *International Journal of Environmental Research and Public Health, 19*(11). http://doi.org/10.3390/ijerph19116877

Menger Leeman, J.M. (2018). *Living our parents' trauma: Effects of child abuse and neglect on the next generation.* [Doctoral dissertation, Australian Catholic University]. https://doi.org/10.4226/66/5a9dbe053362a

Oliver, C. (2020). Inclusive foster care: How foster parents support cultural and relational connections for Indigenous children. *Child & Family Social Work 25*(3), 585-593. https://doi.org/10.1111/cfs.12730

Quinn, A.L.(2022) Experiences and well-being among Indigenous former youth in care within Canada. *Child Abuse & Neglect 123*. https://doi.org/10.1016/j.chiabu.2021.105395

Quinn, A.L. (2020). Nurturing identity among Indigenous youth in care. *Child & Youth Services, 41*(1), 83-104. https://doi: 10.1080/0145935X.2019.1656063

Schmid, J., & Morgenshtern, M. (2022). In history's shadow: Child welfare discourses regarding Indigenous communities in the Canadian social work journal. *International Journal of Child, Youth and Family Studies 13*(1), 145–168. http://doi.org/10.18357/ijcyfs131202220662

Walker, M. (1999). The inter-generational transmission of trauma: The effects of abuse on their survivor's relationship with their children and on the children themselves. *European Journal of Psychotherapy, Counselling and Health, 2*(3), 281–296. http://doi.org/10.1080/13642539908400813

Chapter 3 – The Gift of Feelings

Grosse, G., Streubel, B., Gunzenhauser, C., & Henrik, S. (2021). Let's talk about emotions: The development of children's emotion vocabulary from 4 to 11 years of age. *Affective Science 2*, 150-162. https://doi.org/10.1007/s42761-021-00040-2

Jewell, C., Wittkowski, A., & Pratt, D. (2022). The impact of parent-only interventions on child anxiety: A systematic review and meta-analysis. *Journal of Affective Disorders, 309*, 324-349. https://doi.org/10.1016/j.jad.2022.04.082

Nook, E. C., Stavish, C. M., Sasse, S. F., Lambert, H. K., Mair, P., McLaughlin, K. A., & Somerville, L. H. (2020). Charting the development of emotion comprehension and abstraction from childhood to adulthood using observer-rated and linguistic measures. *Emotion, 20*(5), 773–792. https://doi.org/10.1037/emo0000609

Palmer, P. (1983). *Liking myself*. Impact Publishers.

Randye, J., & Semple, J.L. (2014). Mindfulness-based cognitive therapy for children. In R. Baer (Ed.), *Clinician's guide to evidence base and applications: Practical resources for the mental health professional* (2nd ed., pp 161-188). Academic Press. https://doi.org/10.1016/B978-0-12-416031-6.00008-6

Chapter 4 – When Someone Hurts You

Bailey, C., Knight, T., Koolmatrie, J., Brubacher, S., & Powell, M. (2018). Indigenous perspectives on operation RESET: An initiative to improve the identification and prosecution of child sexual abuse incidents in remote Indigenous communities. *Australian Psychologist 54*(3), 157-234. https://doi.org/10.1111/ap.12349

Bigfoot, D. S., & Braden, J. (2007). Adapting evidence-based treatments for use with American Indian and Native Alaskan children & youth. *Focal Point 21* (1), 19-22. https://www.pathwaysrtc.pdx.edu/pdf/fpW0706.pdf

Bigfoot, D. S., & Schmidt, S. R. (2010). Honouring children, mending the circle: Cultural adaptation of trauma-focused cognitive-behavioral therapy for American Indian and Alaska Native children. *Journal of Clinical Psychology, 66*, 847-856. https://oklahomatfcbt.org/wp-content/uploads/2020/09/Adapting-TF-CBT-for-AI-AN-Children.pdf

Fairholm, J., Fearn, T., & Ross, K., (2013). *Walking the prevention circle: Our children our future for Aboriginal communities.* (3rd Ed). Canadian Red Cross.

Jaramillo, J., Mello, A.R., & Worrell, F.C. (2015). Ethnic identity, stereotype threat, and perceived discrimination among Native American adolescents, *Journal of Research on Adolescence, 10*, 769-775. 1111/jora.12228, 26, 4, (769-775)

Payne D, Olson K, & Parrish J.W. (2013). Pathway to hope: An Indigenous approach to healing child sexual abuse. *International Journal of Circumpolar Health 72*(1). http://doi.org/10.3402/ijch.v72i0.21067

Chapter 5 – Unhealthy Ways of Expressing Your Hurt and Upset Feelings

Liu F, Gao C, Gao H, & Liu W. (2022). The automatic emotion regulation of children aged 8-12: An ERP study. *Front Behavioral Neuroscience 16*, 384-394. http://doi.org/10.3389/fnbeh.2022.921802

Maughan A., & Cicchetti, D. (2002). Impact of child maltreatment and inter-adult violence on children's emotion regulation abilities and socioemotional adjustment. *Child Development 73*(5), 1525-1543. http://doi:10.1111/1467-8624.00488

Leuzinger-Bohleber, M. (2014). Social emotional risk factors. *Child Indicators Research, 7*(4), 715-734. http://doi.org/10.007/s12187-014-9261-7

Tichon, J. G. (2015). Exploring how children express feelings and emotions in an online support group. *Computers in Human Behavior, 53*, 469-474. https://doi.org/10.1016/j.chb.2015.07.013

Zeman, J., & Garber, J. (1996). Display rules for anger, sadness, and pain: It depends on who is watching. *Child Development, 67*(3), 957–973. https://doi.org/10.2307/1131873Top of Form

Chapter 6 – Healthy Ways of Expressing Your Hurt and Upset Feelings

Jewell, C., Wittkowski, A., & Pratt, D. (2022). The impact of parent-only interventions on child anxiety: A systematic review and meta-analysis. *Journal of Affective Disorders, 309*, 324-349. https://doi.org/10.1016/j.jad.2022.04.082

Flanagan, R., & Symonds, J. E. (2022). Children's self-talk in naturalistic classroom settings in middle childhood: A systematic literature review. *Educational Research Review, 35*(3). http://doi:10.1016/j.edurev.2022.100432

Kucirkova N. (2019). How could children's storybooks promote empathy? A conceptual framework based on developmental psychology and literary theory. *Frontiers in Psychology, 10*(121), 1-15. https://www.ncbi.nlm.nih.gov/pmc/articles/PMC6370723/

Li, P. (2023). *Emotional regulation in children: A complete guide.* Parenting for brain. https://www.parentingforbrain.com/self-regulation-toddler-temper-tantrums/

Pelini, S. (2017). *Teaching your child to manage anger and anxiety.* Raising independent kids: Transforming research into practical tools and resources. https://raising-independent-kids.com/1163-2/

Rouse, M.H. (2023). *How can we help kids with self regulation? Some kids need help learning to control their emotions and resist impulsive behavior.* Child Mind Institute. https://childmind.org/bio/matthew-h-rouse-phd-msw/

Vasilopoulos, F., & Ellefson, M.R. (2021). Investigation of the associations between physical activity, self-regulation, and educational outcomes in childhood. *Public Library of Science 16*(5). https://doi.org/10.1371/journal.pone.0250984

Weir, K. (2023, January 11). *How to help kids understand and manage their emotions: Parents, teachers, and other caregivers have an important role in teaching children self-regulation.* American Psychological Association. https://www.apa.org/topics/parenting/emotion-regulation

Zimmer-Gembeck, M. J., Rudolph, J., Kerin, J., & Bohadana-Brown, G. (2022). Parent emotional regulation: A meta-analytic review of its association with parenting and child adjustment. *International Journal of Behavioral Development, 46*(1), 63-82. https://doi.org/10.1177/01650254211051086

Chapter 7 – When Someone You Know has an Addiction to Alcohol, Drugs, Pills, or Other Substances

Alberta Health Services, Alberta Addictions and Mental Health Research (2018). *Solvents/inhalants information for health professionals.* https://crismprairies.ca/wp-content/uploads/2018/12/Solvents Inhalants_V02-2018-11-13.pdf

Ariel, R., & Ariel, L. R. (2022) Opioid use in Indigenous populations: Indigenous perspectives and directions in culturally responsive care. *Journal of Social Work Practice in the Addictions 22*(3), 255-263. https://doi.org/10.1080/1533256X.2022.2049161

Bisaga, A., and Chernyaev, K. (2018). *Overcoming opioid addiction: The authoritative medical guide for patients, families, doctors, and therapists*. The Experiment, LLC.

Brockie, T.N., Campbell, J.C., Dana-Sacco, G., Farley, J., Belcher, H.M., Kub, J., Nelson, K.E., Ivanich, J.D., Yang, L., Wallen, G., Wetsit, L., & Wilcox, H.C. (2022). Protection from polysubstance use among Native American adolescents and young adults. *Prevention Science, 23*, 1287-1298. https://doi.org/10.1007/s11121-022-01373-5

Heavyrunner-Rioux A.R., & Hollist, D.R. (2010). Community, family, and peer influences on alcohol, marijuana, and illicit drug use among a sample of Native American youth: An analysis of predictive factors. *Journal of Ethnic Substance Abuse, 9*(4), 260-283. http://doi:10.1080/15332640.2010.522893

Maina, G., Mclean, M., Mcharo, S., Kennedy, M., Djiometio, J., & King, A. A. (2020). Scoping review of school-based Indigenous substance use prevention in preteens (7-13 years). *Substance Abuse Treatment and Prevention Policy, 15*. http://doi.org/10.1186/s13011-020-00314-1

Proctor, A. L., & McCollum, C. (2018). *Perceptions of methamphetamine in Indian country: Interviews with service providers in ten western tribes*. Department of Justice, Office of Community Oriented Policing Services. https://catalog.library.vanderbilt.edu/discovery/fulldisplay/alma991043541343303276/01VAN_INST:vanui

Soto C., West A., Unger J., et al. (2019). *Addressing the opioid crisis in American Indian & Alaska Native communities in California: A statewide needs assessment*. University of California. https://ipr.usc.edu/wp-content/uploads/2019/11/USC_AI_Report.pdf

Yasmin, L., Hurd, O., Manzoni, M., Pletnikoy, V., Francis. S., Sagnik Bhattacharyya., & Melis, M. (2019). Cannabis and the developing brain: Insights into its long-lasting effects. *Journal of Neuroscience, 39*(42), 8250-8258. https://doi.org/10.1523/JNEUROSCI

Wellbriety Movement (2020). About Us. *Wellbriety teachings.* http://wellbriety.com/about-us/

Zapolski, T.C., Fisher, S., Banks, D.E., Hensel, D.J., & Barnes-Najor, J. (2017). Examining the protective effect of ethnic identity on drug attitudes and use among a diverse youth population. *Journal of Youth and Adolescence, 46*, 1702-1715. http://doi.ort/10.1007/s10964-016-0605-0

Chapter 8 — When Someone You Know Passes Away

Anderson, M., & Woticky, G. (2018). The end of life is an auspicious opportunity for healing: Decolonizing death and dying for urban Indigenous people. *International Journal of Indigenous Health, 13*(2),48-60. http://doi.org/10.18357/ijih.v13i2.32062

Ansloos, J. (2018). Rethinking Indigenous Suicide. *International Journal of Indigenous Health, 13*(2),8-28. http://doi.org/10.18357/ijih.v13i2.32061

Eklund, R., Alvariza, A., Kreicbergs, U., Jalmsell, L., & Lovgren, M. (2020). The family talk intervention for families when a parent is cared for in palliative care, potential effects from minor children's perspectives. *BMC Palliative Care,19.* https://doi.org/10.1186/s12904-020-00551-y

Gibson, M., Stuart, J., Leske, Raelene Ward, L., & Vidyattama, Y. (2021). Does community cultural connectedness reduce the influence of area disadvantage on Aboriginal & Torres Strait Islander young peoples' suicide? *Australian and New Zealand Journal of Public Health, 45*(6), 643-650. https://doi.org/10.1111/1753-6405.13164

Haine, R.A., Ayers, T.S., Sandler, I.N., & Wolchik, S.A. (2008). Evidence-based practices for parentally bereaved children and their families. *Professional Psychology: Research and Practice, 39*(2):113-121. http://doi.org/10.1037/0735-7028.39.2.113

Heart, B., & DeBruyn, L. M. (1998). The American Indian holocaust: Healing historical unresolved grief. *American Indian and Alaska Native Mental Health Research, 8*(2), 56-78. https://pubmed.ncbi.nlm.nih.gov/9842066/

Krone, A. (2016). *Loss, Grief, & Children in Care*. Manitoba Office of the Children's Advocate. Canada. https://policycommons.net/artifacts/2009516/loss-grief-children-in-care/2761959/

Longbottom S., & Slaughter, V. (2018). Sources of children's knowledge about death and dying. *The Royal Society Publishing, Biological Sciences, 373*(1754). http://doi.org/10.1098/rstb.2017.0267

Menendez, D., Hernandez, I., & Rosengren, K.S. (2020). Children's emerging understanding of death. *Child Developmental Perspectives, 14*(1). http://doi.org/10.1111/cdep.12357

Poonwassie, A. (2006). Grief and trauma in Aboriginal communities in Canada. *International Journal of Health Promotion and Education, 44*, 29-33. https://doi.org/10.1080/14635240.2006.10708062

Simpson, J. (2020). *I lost my family: Grief, loss, and identity formation of fostered and adopted American Indian individuals* (Masters theses, Virginia Polytechnic Institute and State University). Virginia Tech. https://vtechworks.lib.vt.edu/handle/10919/99052?show=full

Chapter 9 – Taking Care of Your Spirit: Your Mind, Your Body, and Your Heart

Absolon, K. (2010). Indigenous wholistic theory: A knowledge set for practice. *First Peoples Child & Family Review,5*, 73-87. https://doi.org/10.7202/1068933ar

Ahmed F., Liberda E.N., Solomon A., Davey R., Sutherland B., & Tsuji, L.J. (2023). Indigenous land-based approaches to well-being: The niska (goose) harvesting program in subarctic Ontario, Canada.

International Journal of Environmental Research and Public Health, 19. https://tspace.library.utoronto.ca/bitstream/1807/126679/1/ijerph-20-03686-v2.pdf

Ahmed F., Zuk A.M., & Tsuji L.J.S. (2021). The impact of land-based physical activity interventions on self-reported health and well-being of Indigenous adults: A systematic review. *International Journal of Environmental Research and Public Health, 18.* http://doi.org/10.3390/ijerph18137099

Brown, H. J., McPherson, G., Peterson, R., Newman, V., & Cranner, B. (2012). Our land, our language: Connecting dispossession and health equity in an Indigenous context. *Canadian Journal of Nursing Research, 44*(2), 44-63. https://pubmed.ncbi.nlm.nih.gov/22894006/

Hart, M. A. (2007). *Seeking mino-pimatisiwin: An Aboriginal approach to helping.* Fernwood.

Kral, M.J., Idlout, L., Minore, J.B., Dyck, R.J., & Kirmayer, L.J. (2011). Unikkaartuit: Meanings of well-being, unhappiness, health, and community change among Inuit in Nunavut, Canada. *American Journal of Community Psychology, 48*(3-4),426-38. http://doi: 10.1007/s10464-011-9431-4. PMID: 21387118.

Lafrance, J. (2013). *A time for atonement: "At-one-moment — to be of one mind".* iUniverse.

Markstrom, C. A., & Moilanen, K. L. (2016). School, community, and cultural connectedness as predictors of adjustment among rural American Indian/Alaska Native (AI/AN) adolescents. In L. J. Crockett & G. Carlo (Eds.), *Rural ethnic minority youth and families in the United States: Theory, research, and applications* (pp. 109–126). Springer International Publishing/Springer Nature. https://doi.org/10.1007/978-3-319-20976-0_7

Priest, N., Mackean, T., Davis, E., Briggs, L., & Waters, E. (2012) Aboriginal perspectives of child health and wellbeing in an urban setting: Developing a conceptual framework. *Health Sociology Review, 21*(2), 180-195. http://doi.org/10.5172/hesr.2012.21.2.180

Ross, R., (2014). *Indigenous healing: Exploring traditional paths.* Penguin Books Ltd.

Ullrich, J. S. (2019). For the love of our children: An Indigenous connectedness framework. *AlterNative: An International Journal of Indigenous Peoples, 15*(2), 121-130. https://journals.sagepub.com/doi/10.1177/1177180119828114

Chapter 10 — Conclusion and Being Proud of Your Native Identity

Allison-Burbank, J.D., & Reid, T. (2023). Prioritizing connectedness and equity in speech-language services for American Indian and Alaska Native children. *Language, Speech, and Hearing Services in Schools, 54*(2), 368-374. http://doi.org/10.1044/2022_LSHSS-22-00101.

Brave Heart, M. Y., Chase, J., Elkins, J., & Altschul, D. B. (2011). Historical trauma among Indigenous peoples of the Americas: Concepts, research, and clinical considerations. *Journal of Psychoactive Drugs, 43*(4), 282-290.

Carolissen, R. L., & Duckett, P. S. (2018). Teaching toward decoloniality in community psychology and allied disciplines: Editorial introduction. *American Journal of Community Psychology, 62*(3-4), 241-249. http://doi.org/10.1002.ajcp.12297

Castagno, A. E., & Brayboy, B. M. J. (2008). Culturally responsive schooling for Indigenous youth: A review of the literature. *Review of Educational Research, 78*(4), 941-993.

Fitzgerald, H. E., Johnson, D. J., Qin, D. B., Villarruel, F. A., & Norder, J. (Eds.). (2019). *Handbook of children and prejudice: Integrating research, practice, and policy.* Springer.

Iruka, I. U., Gardner-Neblett, N., Telfer, N. A., Ibekwe-Ibekwe, N., Curenton, S. M., Sims, J., Sansbury, A. B., & Neblettm E. W. (2022). Effects of racism on child development: Advancing antiracist developmental science. *Annual Review of Developmental Psychology, 4*(1), 109-132. http://doi.org/10.1146/annurev-devpsych-121020-031339

Macedo, D. M., Smithers, L. G., Roberts, R. M., Haag, D. G., Paradies, Y., & Jamieson, L. M. (2019). Does ethnic-racial identity modify the effects of racism on the social the social and emotional wellbing of Aboriginal Australian children? *Public Library of Science.* http://doi.org/10.137/journal.pone0220744

Middleton-Moz, J., Mishna, F., Martell, R., Williams, C., & Samar, Z (2021). Indigenous trauma and resilience: pathways to "bridging the river" in social work education. *Social Work Education.* http://doi.org/10.1080/02615479.2021.1998427

Mutuyimanam, C., & Maercker, A. (2023). Clinically relevant historical trauma sequelae: A systematic review. *Clinical Psychology & Psychotherapy, 30*(2). http://doi.org/10.1002.cpp.2836

Saleem, F. T., & Anderson, R. E. (2020). Addressing the "myth" of racial trauma: Developmental and ecological considerations for youth of colour. *Clinical Child and Family Psychology Review, 23*(1), 1-14. http://doi.org/10.1007/s10567-019-00304-1

Waldram, J. B. (1997). *The way of the pipe: Aboriginal spirituality and symbolic healing in Canadian prisons.* Broadview Press.

Waldram, J. B. (2004). *Revenge of the windigo: The construction of the mind and mental health of North American Aboriginal peoples.* University of Toronto Press.

ABOUT THE AUTHOR

Geraldine (Geri) Paul (Ootskwi Papoom Akii) grew up in a traditional hunting and fishing community in Labrador, Canada. She is of Inuit descent from her mother's family (Hazel Kippenhuck; Samuel and Madeline Kippenhuck; Nellie Parr, Labrador). Geri is also of Mi'kmaq descent from her father's family (Gerald Paul; Thomas and Beatrice Paul; Abraham and Margaret Paul, from Wigwam Point, NF).

Geri is a registered psychologist who works exclusively with Indigenous people. She has worked in private practice for many years, and has extensive experience working in various Native agencies, universities, colleges, and Native communities. Geri graduated from the University of Calgary with her Master of Science degree and Bachelor of Arts (Honours) degree. She also has numerous diplomas and certificates. Geri's understanding and firsthand experiences of racism, oppression, and neocolonialism inspire her to continue helping Native people.

She has three adult daughters (Amanda, Chelsy, and Tory) and one *amazing* grandson (Tarek). Geri lives with her husband near the Standoff reserve in Alberta. She also spends her time on the Blackfeet reservation in Montana. Being active in Native culture and ceremonies is central to Geri's identity and happiness. You can reach Geri at interact.services@yahoo.com

www.ingramcontent.com/pod-product-compliance
Lightning Source LLC
Chambersburg PA
CBHW081104080526
44587CB00021B/3444